Humorous Middles

Musings by
R. K. Murthi

Published by:

F-2/16, Ansari road, Daryaganj, New Delhi-110002
23240026, 23240027 • *Fax:* 011-23240028
Email: info@vspublishers.com • *Website:* www.vspublishers.com

Regional Office : Hyderabad
5-1-707/1, Brij Bhawan (Beside Central Bank of India Lane)
Bank Street, Koti, Hyderabad - 500 095
040-24737290
E-mail: vspublishershyd@gmail.com

Branch Office : Mumbai
Godown # 34 at The Model Co-Operative Housing, Society Ltd.,
"Sahakar Niwas", Ground Floor, Next to Sobo Central, Mumbai - 400 034
022-23510736
E-mail vspublishersmum@gmail.com

Follow us on:

All books available at **www.vspublishers.com**

© Copyright: V&S PUBLISHERS
ISBN 978-93-813847-6-3

This book was earlier printed in the name of *Quick Bites for spare moments.*

The Copyright of this book, as well as all matter contained herein (including illustrations) rests with the Publisher. No person shall copy the name of the book, its title design, matter and illustrations in any form and in any language, totally or partially or in any form. Anybody doing so shall face legal action and will be responsible for damages.

Printed at : Param Offseters Okhla New Delhi-110020

Preface 7

Better Half and Bitter Half   9

    What's in the pot?   11
    Ugly husband, wife's delight   13
    On memory lapses   15
    Surprise gift   17
    Credit-worthy husband!   23
    Doe   26
    Tit for tat   29
    Psychological muddle   32
    Don't ask for the moon   37
    All 'keyed' up!   39
    Riding the storm   41
    Dutch wife   44
    Flying missiles   47
    Neurotic over a stapler   49

Potshots at Oneself   51

Anti-hero   53
Buttoned out   55
What have I written?   57
Waterloo   59
Tailor's dummy   61
Tie or choker   63
Playing the critic   65
For whom belloc tolls   67
I pick pockets   69
Mirrors make the twain meet   71
Charge of the grey brigade   73
Fuzzy logic   75
Defending poor memory   77
A form of inspiration   79
Man in the rut   82

Perky Profiles   85

Remote control   87
The better half   90
Dictator's delight   93
Bull in a China shop   96

Travel Travail   99

The last laugh   101
The roofless lady   103

Travel trouble   105
Camera-shy   107
Identity check   110
Malayan wisdom   113
A victorian tale   116
Tongue-twister   118
Talk over   120

Random Reflections   123

In praise of the kerchief   125
Palm-top legacy   127
A haunting mystery   129
Let judges court rhyme   131
Musical chairs   133
Principles and man   135
Cross thoughts   137
On windows   139
Ban the back pocket   141
Speech is golden   145
The meek do not inherit the earth   148
Bridges: Concrete and conceptual   151
On eyebrows   154
Dating diary gives the jitters   157
Ifs and buts of History   161
Relativity   163
Critics, authors and artists   166
Caught on the wrong foot   169

Dogs beware   172
Thumbs up!   175
Orators and hecklers   179
The cryptic art   181
The automatic watch   183
Symbol of gratitude   185
The farce of form-filling   187
Late to rise   190
Strange reasons   192
Second fiddle   195

Amusing Encounters   197

Value of a tip   199
Apparatchik   201
Tit for tat   203
Water on the rocks!   205
Obviously yours   207
Fattening thoughts   210
Clock watch   213
Silencing the wag   216
For friendship's sake   219
Right logic   222

◆◆◆

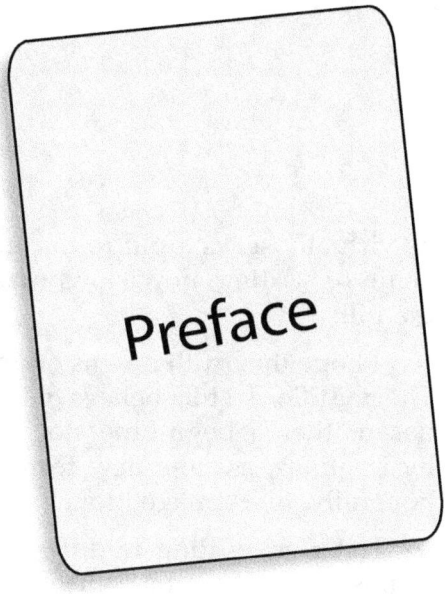

Once upon a time, the middle had a pride of place in almost every major newspaper. It was right at the centre of the edit page. Other sombre or thought-provoking or scholarly articles acted, in a way, as maids in waiting to the middle. The middle was looked upon as the midriff, the backbone of the edit page.

I started writing middles in that golden age when the middle was duly accorded the place consistent with its title.

Good times, it is said, never lasts. The middle enjoys hardly any privileged slot now. Many newspapers have cut down on the frequency of the middle from six days a week to two or three. Even when it appears, it has been demoted to the bottom right corner or the bottom left corner. Thus has the middle been cornered, pushed to the edge. Now, it won't need much of a strong push to throw the middle out. So I, for one, won't be surprised if the middle joins the dodo in the none-too distant future. I draw solace from the philosophy, *Life is transient, so why should a genre of creative writing like the middle not find itself put away as not suited to the new age?*

Not that this augurs well for the future. Man doesn't live by bread alone. He needs butter and honey and biscuits and choice drinks too. The middle, along with the short story and the poems, provides just the diversion the reader needed. Having mopped up the terrible tales of tragedies and disheartening reports of the ugly deals of politicians and the mess, the world leaders have made of our earth, he virtually seeks a pill to dispel the pain within. Literary genre of writing, now slowly fading out, play the role of the pill.

I hope this truth dawns on the readers, sooner or later. The middle, I still, believe will survive. For the middle has neither a beginning nor an end. It may take new incarnations, assume new formats, but it will be around, hopefully, till Armageddon.

I started writing middles around 1960. The middles in this collection, (the fourth such collections), have been extracted from leading English language publications including *The Times of India, The Hindustan Times, The Tribune, The Indian Express, The Deccan Herald, The Evening News, The Statesman, The Pioneer, The Patriot, Femina* and *Eve's Weekly*. In these middles, I have spared none. I have been as much the target of my witty digs as others.

It is my fervent hope that this collection will be as well received as the previous ones.

Better Half
and
Bitter Half

What's in the pot?

My wife is stirring the mashed ingredients, submerged in water and held in a pot that gets the heat from the bottom, with a spoon. I get a whiff of the exotic smell and ask her, "What's the pot boiler of the day?" There goes the writer in you, says my better half. "I am not going anywhere till I know what is cooking?" I dig in my heels. "Go and produce a potboiler, try to hit the jackpot. Take a potshot at potluck. This is the best of time for Indian writers. Heard of Manil Suri or Jumpa Lahiri or ...! They hit the jackpot with their potboilers," the lady fires at me a virtual who-is-who of terms that are rooted in the word POT. "So my skill at playing with words has rubbed on to you", I mildly reprove her for trying to steal my thunder. "Words are not your monopoly," she gives an extra churning to the mix of tomatoes and green chilly and tamarind pulp and salt and the intoxicating smell of *rasam* hits my olfactory organ. "So I can't even file a case against you before the Monopoly Commission," I joke. "You are barking at the wrong pot," my wife parodies an idiom that talks about barking at the wrong tree. "Go and fire your creativity. Set its bottom, wherever it be, on fire". "Why do you want the bottom to be set on fire?" I ask.

"Elementary, my dear! The pot boils only when its bottom is set on fire. The rocket takes to flight only when its bottom is on fire. Your imagination will fly high only when it is forced to drag its seat away from the scalding heat," my wife shares her understanding of where the heat needs to be selectively applied. "It is not as easy as all that, dear. The path of creativity is often littered with potholes," I find the right POT word. "Is not a POT a hole? A hole with no hole at the bottom, so it becomes a one-way street to whatever one wants to boil in the pot?" she jokes. "My God! Potholes are what litter a bad road," I clarify. "As if I don't know!" she ticks me off before continuing, "Have you heard of pot wrestlers?" "Do wrestlers fight for pots?" I make light of her statement. "They do. One who wins the pot gets the dish the pot contains, when it is fresh and hot and truly delicious. He has his first fill. Others wait for their turns. Strange that he is usually the one who doesn't have a potbelly. Others display varying patterns of bulging tummies and resultant slowness when it comes to wrestling it out for the pot." "Are there a few more pot shots in your armoury? "I have half a mind to use a term that shows the target's intelligence in poor light," she laughs, leaving it to me to guess the word, CRACKPOT. Suddenly, it dawns on me. I have enough material for a skit. So I hurry out, ready to churn out a potboiler with words.

Uglyhusband, wife's delight

The signal the receding hairline sends out to my wife is clear. She realises that my top is trying to shape itself into an egghead. I know that every egghead is not an intellectual. I have no pretensions on that count. So when I end up displaying a head that reminds everyone of a billiard ball, I shall still remember that I fall short of the highest standards of intellectual rating by quite a few notches. "Oh! How smart you looked, with those curly hair, glossy, wavy, when we got married! I almost thought you were cupid!" my wife groans. "Don't be stupid," I find a rhyming word, before continuing, "Be happy that I am heading towards a hairless top. Soon if I gain enough wisdom, people may call me a modern day Socrates? And if I become a nuisance, they may force me to keep a date with hemlock," I banter. "Can you be serious for once? Why don't you seek pomades and lotions, try hair transplant, if necessary, to arrest the hair fall," she looks at me wistfully. "And end up a pauper? Have you any idea how much it costs to buy these cures about whose efficacy I have reservations?" I point out. "Oh, if only I can put the clock back!" my wife sighs.

"Don't chase impossible dreams. Instead find the positive notes that my impending state of baldness strikes, the safety and security that come with it," I take a breather. "Positive notes? Where do you find them?" my wife is sceptical. "I will help you find them," I hold out hopes. "Out with your offbeat ideas, then," my wife reluctantly lets me have my say. "Bald men are rarely ever considered super smart.

Once I am bald, no wily young woman, looking for suitable husband material, shall consider me smart enough to throw a bait in my direction," I tell her. "My God!" "If I grow fat and stout and develop a big spread round the waist, you can feel safer. When I sport wrinkles on the face and the crow's feet etch dark shadows below the eyes, you can feel absolutely certain that our marriage will never be rocked by illicit relationship," I joke. "Is it your contention that a wife is secure only if her man is..." "Taller, older, heavier, uglier and hoarser, says EW Howe," I chuckle, draw my wife closer and whisper in her ears, "Love me now for what I am today. On every passing day, you will find in me a man, with a new face, with lesser hair on top, who loves you and expects you to love him. Variety is the spice of life, dear. With me changing the look of my head everyday, you will never face paucity of spice," I close on finding my wife laughing her head off.

On memory lapses

I admit I suffer from occasional memory lapses. More often than not, they occur when I will them to be so. That may sound odd, but there is a logic behind my claim. Usually, I keep memory lapses under check, collared and pinioned and trussed up, held out of harm's way, behind bars, in the locked cells of my mind. There they stay, pickled, restless, perhaps, livid with rage at being denied the opportunity to be free and unfettered. Slavery, I confess, has never reached the abysmal depths to which I have pushed mental lapses. But then I have my interests; and they have to be protected. Memory lapses protect my interests. That is why I keep them, hold them in chains, have them at my beck and call.

Give them an inch and they gain the power of banana peels. One false step and the memory lapses make me slip and fall in a trice. So I hardly ever give anyone of them more than a millimetre. That too under severely controlled conditions! When do I give the memory lapses minimal freedom? The answer is plain and simple. I give them freedom when it is to my advantage. That is when I need the right excuse for my alleged failures. Then I put the blame on memory lapses, make them play the role of sacrificial goats.

Take, for instance, my failure to fetch a gift for my wife on her birthday. I return home, walk in and the first thing I sight is the cake sitting on the dining table. My wife is wearing a fine *Kanjeevaram* saree.

Both my son and daughter, dressed in their very best, hover around the table, licking their lips just waiting for the cake to be cut and distributed.

"Ah, dear," I gently press my wife's palm.

"That is just a verbal gift," my wife scowls.

"I am a man of words," I spar.

"Words can't clothe or feed or satisfy me, now," my wife scowls.

"Sorry, dear. I forgot that today is your birthday," I give the millimetre of space for my memory lapses to come out of their prisons and take the blame on their shoulders.

"Some day, you may even forget me," she is ready to sob.

"Oh, no, this Sunday, we shall go to the market. You may buy whatever you want," I tell her.

The smile returns to her face while I lash out at my failing memory, accuse it of letting me down through its lapses. My memory cells shout and scream, make futile bids to tell my wife that I am feigning memory lapse because I don't have the funds to fetch her a gift, right away, but the language they speak is Greek and Latin to my wife and my children too. They have served their purpose. So quickly I chain them and lead them to their cells and keep them under lock and key, to be aired again when I need them to be the sacrificial goats.

It is a very pleasant November evening. I suggest to my wife that we drive down to Connaught Place. She looks up, unsure of whether she had heard me right. She feels there is a catch somewhere. She does not know what it is. But she knows for certain that it is uncharacteristic of me. Rarely, ever do I come up with such suggestions. That is why she feels a little unsure whether she heard me right.

"You heard me right, dear. Let us drive down to Connaught Place. Let us go window shopping. There is no greater pleasure than that. You don't have to spend a paisa. Yet, you can savour the good things of life. You can stand and stare at attractive models, colourfully draped, stacked away behind glass panes, looking life-like even though they are just made out of mud and paint. You can browse around, pick up books from the shelves, feel the gloss and glamour of good books. You can try shoes or *chappals*, just for the heck of it, and then walk away, saying that the price is too high or the quality is just not good enough for you or you will return after trying at a few more places. Yes, let us go. But, remember, it is the end of the month. So there simply is no cash to buy anything. The only luxury we can afford is some snacks and ice creams at any place you choose. I hope you understand ...." I drop off, looking up to my wife to see the reaction.

She is elated. She nods her head. She hurries to the dressing table, starts uncoiling her hair to set it again. I watch her trimming herself up. I admire her reflection in the mirror. She notes what I am doing and quips, "Hey be careful. Don't fall in love with my mirror image." I chide, "When I have the original, all to myself, why should I fall for the image which is transient, has no existence of its own, projects itself only so long as you stand before the mirror".

My wife laughs. Then she applies pomades, talcum, cream and a lot of other things, runs the comb through her hair, sticks them with pins and needles, wraps a sari with ease, dons a matching blouse and turns to me. She looks really charming. "I now know that make-up can make even an ordinary lass look exotic." My wife curls her lips in displeasure. She is not pleased. I know that. I tell her, "Just in fun, darling. Don't take it seriously. You are a lovely girl. I am glad I own you."

"Own me. I am not a thing to be owned. I am a living, pulsating human being with a mind of my own."

"I mean you are mine, as much as I am yours," I mollify her before starting off towards the scooter. My wife locks the door and joins me. She sits on the pillion seat and we move off. Soon we are at the shopping arcade of Connaught Place. I park the scooter. Then we head towards the inner circle of the shopping arcade.

As we walk, hand in hand, we get a whiff of *agarbati*, and notice a pavement vendor displaying his wares. I refuse to buy from him. I am sceptical. I know one thing about these pavement sellers. They have a way of taking a customer for a ride easily. Or there is some miracle which makes the *agarbati* smell exotic when the vendor lights it, yet it turns odourless, once I take it home. It is the same with the violin which has just three strings, and manages to produce the latest filmi song when handled by the vendor, but produces only catty squeals when I try to play on it.

These thoughts fill my mind when I realise that my wife is not by my side. I turn. I notice her, standing before a glass pane, almost tall enough to accommodate a six-footer. Behind the glass pane is a model, draped in a lovely sari. My wife has eyes only for the sari. She is lost in it. I get close to her, ask her, "Like it, dear."

"Like it. That is an understatement. It is the most lovely sari I have seen in recent months. I wish I could buy it," my wife says.

"Oh, no. We came window shopping. That is all what we will do. But, no harm going in and asking the price. We may also check up whether the shop has saris of the same texture with different colour combinations. Let us have some fun, dear. Just fun. No purchases. I don't have cash. Right!" I tell her while leading her in.

My wife is not exactly pleased. But she has no alternative. For she had agreed to the terms set out at the start. I had told her we would just go around, enjoy looking at things. That is all. Nothing more.

The salesman greets us with a big, broad smile. A ready-made smile, which all salesmen have. They can switch it on or off at will, I think. That is what makes them salesmen. Blue-blooded ones at that.

The salesman waits while I tell him about the sari displayed at the shop window. "You must have other colour combinations of the sari. I would like to see all the variations. Then I would like to decide," I hold out a vague hint that I might make a purchase.

That sets the salesman into motion. He leads me and my wife to the corner where a dozen saris, which belong to the variety which had caught our eyes, are stacked in a shelf. He pulls them out, one by one, opens them, holds out the *pallav*, lets us take a look at the exotic prints, rolls along merrily, focussing attention on the plus points of each sari. My wife waits till her eyes land on a light blue sari. It has a dark border. The *pallav* looks immaculate. I notice the glint in her eyes. I know for certain that she has fallen for it.

The salesmen too is quick to notice that my wife has lost her heart to the sari. He smiles and says, "Good one, Madam. I admire your taste. Only the other day, Mrs X, (He drops the name of a well-known dancer) bought three of them. Then there was the diplomat's wife who took two, one for herself and one for her friend. The diplomat was from Singapore. A naturalised Singapore Indian ...."

My wife does not even look at me. Instead, she feels the texture while enquiring from the salesman what the price of the sari is. He turns the sari around, spots the price tag and reads out, "Rs 1475/-", "Taxes", he says, are extra.

"Too high," I mumble.

The salesman peers at me, half in contempt, says, "Sir, good stuff is always costly. This is a collector's item, mind you".

I sternly tell my wife, "Ah, darling... Come. The price is too high."

The salesman looks beaten. My wife looks crest-fallen. But there is precious little that she can do. She reluctantly trails behind me. I wave to the salesman and say, "Maybe, I will be back soon." He does not take me seriously. He realises he has wasted his energies. He thinks my wife and I have just walked in to look at things.

My wife is glum for about ten minutes. Then she says, "Wish I could have that sari. Did you see how well the blue body fits in with the black border and the printed *pallav*. I wish I could own it. But, then, I know... I know this is the end of the month and we can't buy it ...."

I lead her to a restaurant. We sit down to eat *masala dosa* and ice cream.

We loaf around and window shop before returning home late.

A few days later comes my wife's birthday.

I return home early, carrying with me a lovely present for her. It is packed, neatly. I give it to her. Then I give her a hug and wish her many happy returns of the day. She starts opening the parcel. I tell her, "Wait, darling, guess, what is in it."

"How can 1 guess, when there are so many things you can get as a gift. It could be a cardigan. Or a shawl. Or a bedspread. No, darling. I can't guess," she says.

"I will give you a tip. It is a gift which would please you most. For you had set your heart on it sometime back. I think that should give you a clue as to what is in the parcel," I state enigmatically.

"What could it be .... "My wife scratches her head. She finds it difficult to get at the answer. She pouts her lips and says, "Can't make any progress in this guessing game. Tell me, dear. Tell me, what is in it?"

"Something that will hug you, adjust to your figure, bring out your personality in bold relief. Something that will add to your charm. Something that you will be proud to have," I still gloss over the exact identification of the gift.

"You are rousing my curiosity," she grumbles.

"Curiosity won't kill you, darling. You are not a cat," I snipe in good humour.

"I can't wait a minute," says my wife. She tears the brown paper and pulls out the plastic bag within which lies the prized object. She finally gets hold of the gift. It is the sari on which she had set her heart when I took her to Connaught Place, a few days back. Her eyes bulge out in surprise. She is thrilled. She whirls around, holding the sari, before coming close to me to peck gently on my cheek. I pat her and say, "Do you know dear that I took you out, that day, to Connaught Place, only to find out what gift you would love. I noticed how much you fell for the sari. So the day after our outing, I went to the shop and bought it. And I decided to give it to you as a gift on your birthday."

"Thank you, darling. That is a surprise gift. The best gift you could have given me on this occasion. Oh, how sad I felt that day because I could not get it. And all the time, you were planning to get it for me. You say it is difficult to understand a woman. I say a man is more complex and has many surprises up his sleeves. At least, my man is full of surprises."

"Pleasant ones, darling," I quip and ask my wife when she would give me a piece of cake and a cup of coffee.

Credit-worthy husband!

I TRUDGE back home, after the day's work. I am tired. The whole day, I had plied my way through files, dictated letters to my steno, finalised drafts for the boss, met him to offer clarifications he sought, interacted with customers who had come in with their problems. The return journey, by the Delhi Transport Corporation (DTC). (The chartered bus which I normally take, had given me the slip, without prior warning)... has sapped me of all energy.

The weariness which seeps through me is very much evident when I reach home. My wife is there, beaming a happy smile, dressed neatly, as is her wont, welcoming me, helping me shed some of my tiredness. She takes the briefcase from my hand, gently nudges me to the sofa, waits till I sit down before moving back to the kitchen, saying, "One minute. I shall be back with a cup of coffee."

I lean back in the sofa and grin. I am happy I have a loving wife. Her very presence, I admit, lifts my spirits.

The smell of the beverage hits me even before my wife hands over the steaming cup of coffee to me. She sits by my side and waits for me to taste the drink that cheers.

"Thank you, dear," I tell her.

"Ah.... Today, the vendor from Kashmir, who sells shawls and *phirens* and woollen blouses came," my wife informs me.

"Ah..." I do not say anything more.

"He had some very good items. The price too was cheap. So, I bought a shawl and a *phiren*. I hope you will approve them. I have paid him only Rs 50. I shall pay him the balance..."

"What is the total amount that is to be paid?" I enquire, a sharpness touching my tone.

"The shawl costs Rs 225. The *phiren* costs Rs 250. The total amount is Rs 475," my wife elucidates.

"Ah... you are good at adding," I sneer.

"Thank you," she fails to note that I am far from enthusiastic.

"I don't need thanks. You have already bought the two items. But, where shall the funds come from? You know that we are not that rich that we can afford to buy whatever catches our fancy," I snap.

"My God!" my wife manages to restrain the tears which well up in her eyes.

"God cannot help those who do not help themselves," I snip.

"You mean you don't approve of my purchase. You know I have no shawl. Nor do I have a *phiren*. I have just two sweaters, which I knitted three years back," my wife points out.

"I know. But, where shall the funds come from?" I hold on to my view.

"I don't know. But, I bought the two items because I have faith in you. I have told the vendor that I shall pay the amount in five installments. So, every month, we have to pay Rs 100 or so. That, I think, I can manage," my wife peps me up by saying she has faith in me.

"Aha," I find that there is some substance in her statement.

"So, you agree that I shall keep the items," my wife has a touch of hope on her face.

"All right, dear," I decide not to spoil the evening by further quibbling, when I realise that what she has bought are items which she really needs.

"Thank you... Do you know one thing? When a wife buys things on credit, she is merely displaying confidence in her husband," my wife moves back, lifting the empty cup, while I call to her, "Thank you, dear. I am glad I am worthy of such confidence."

"YOU have stopped calling me Doe," says my wife when we sit at the balcony of our flat, watching the clouds which chase each other, occasionally bumping into each other, sending shafts of light and roars of thunder.

"Ah...There is a valid reason, dear," I tell her.

"You mean my eyes do not remind you, any longer, of the doe? Remember, when we married, that was the first thing you told me. I remember your exact words: *Your eyes, my girl, are like those of a doe*. And often, you would call me, Doe, lending to the term immense love and affection," says my wife, whipping up memories of the first night of married bliss.

"I know, dear. Your eyes still have the flighty grace that I find in the doe. I also know that you are a female, that there is nothing wrong in calling you, Doe. For the Doe is a female deer, while you, my beloved, is my dear female," I respond.

"Yet, you don't call me Doe, any longer. I had assumed that you will use that pet phrase always. Perhaps, two decades of marriage has stilled the fire of love," my wife grumbles, indicating that she wants to be called Doe.

"I do not have the heart to call you Doe any longer," I react.

"But, why?" My wife insists on an answer. "Because the name was taken on by a bloody tyrant. The autocrat who seized power, in a coup, about ten years back. The man, I have in mind is Samuel Doe. He came to power through a bloody coup. And he has now gone out of the scene, after tearing his country, Liberia, to shreds." I reply.

"Aha..."

"The nation was rocked by a civil war, for about eight months, while Samuel Doe refused to abdicate. He let his soldiers run wild. Thousands of innocent people lost their lives, because the crazy Doe wanted to cling on to power. Finally, when he was shot in the leg, captured by his opponents and summarily executed, the people sighed in relief. But, in the process, Doe has sullied the whole clan of Doe, given to the term, 'Doe', bloody connotations," I take a breather.

"My God!"

"Yes, my dear. Nearly six months back, I realised the bloody notes which accompanied the name, Doe. That was when I stopped calling you Doe. For, I did not want your pet name to carry even the slightest touch of the bloody monster. I think I can now resume calling you Doe, now that the wily Doe is dead. The only Doe which is around is the female deer and my own dear female. What do you say, my Doe," I tease her.

"It is nice to be called by that name again," my wife smiles.

"I know. I hold you as my female dear. But there are quite a few men who look upon their better half as Dear Females ....And then they add, with the typically masculine air of superiority, that their wives are truly dear, with their unending desire to be one up on the neighbours and their craving for high living," I throw some light on the term, 'Dear'.

"I hope you are not using the term, 'Female Dear' because you think I burn holes in your budget" my wife asks. "Oh, no. You are indeed a doe, my own gazelle, my own female deer, as also my dear female," I pick up her hand and press it gently.

Ask me who is the greatest menace to the pedestrian and I would unhesitatingly point out the backseat driver, who has the uncanny knack of offering unsolicited warnings and unwanted advice to the man at the steering wheel at inopportune moments. The trouble is that the menace invariably takes the form of the driver's better half (or, is she the bitter half!) I wonder why no law has been passed prohibiting back-seat driving. This is one legislation that should be urgently incorporated into our legal code, if a semblance of orderliness is to be restored on the highways.

I am not speaking casually or cantankerously. Having lived with a lady, (my wife), who is the world's best back-seat driver, I have undergone the travails and agonies of driving. She has the habit of shouting, suddenly, "God. You nearly knocked him down." I would raise my head and shout back, "I thought God is immortal." She would be silenced by this caustic comment, but not for long. She would, almost with a malicious glint in her mischievous eyes, draw my attention to the fact that I was going through a street where vehicular traffic was prohibited. Or, I was in the wrong direction in an one-way alley. She would nudge me to overtake where overtaking is prohibited, tempt me to take the wrong turn, warn me of the red signal at the last moment, do everything in her power to lead me to a state of mental exasperation.

For several years, I had been searching for a panacea for this madness in my wife. The idea suggested Itself, one day, when I was being guided, nay misguided, by my wife while driving through one of the busy, congested lanes of Delhi. I was elated when the remedy struck me at a time when I was at the end of my tether due to back-seat driving. I chuckled to myself. My ruminations were cut short by the back-seat driver.

Next day, I got a chance to carry out my resolution, to give her a dose of the medicine which I hoped would rid her of the mania for back-seat driving. My wife was stitching a blouse when I walked over to her side, pulled a chair and sank into it. I watched her, with a twinkle in my eye. After sometime, I remarked, "Aren't you running the machine a little too fast?" She turned round and gave me an icy stare. I ignored the danger signal that she flashed out through her eyes. After a short pause, I threw in a word of caution. I said, "Mind your fingers." She froze in her seat. With great difficulty, she turned towards me and enquired angrily, "What's wrong with my fingers?" I smiled and replied, "Oh. Nothing. Only you must be careful. Otherwise, you'll find the needle threading your fingers also, sewing them into one compact unit." My wife rasped out like a live bomb, "Thank you. I don't need your advice. I've been stitching on this machine for the last fifteen years."

I smiled, condescendingly, and continued to sit by her side, watching her closely. She was visibly upset by my candid comments. She did not talk to me. When I tried to draw her into conversation, she ignored me and clung to silence. When I prodded her, she replied with snorts and grunts. I felt excited, I was on the road to success.

In the evening, my wife was preparing coffee. I strode into the kitchen and sniffed at the roasted coffee seeds. I shrieked, "You've fried the seeds too much." I surveyed the cake she had just pulled out of the oven and remarked, "You were in a hurry, darling. Otherwise, you should have allowed the cake to remain inside the oven for another ten minutes. Or, did conscience prick you for roasting the cake at such high temperature inside the oven?"

Before I concluded my last comment, my wife exploded, "What's the matter with you? You're offering advice on topics about which you're absolutely ignorant. You don't know even the ABC of sewing, cooking and other domestic activities."

I allowed a sly smile to hang between my lips when I answered with alacrity, "That's no reason why I shouldn't offer some suggestions. I thought it only fair to help you, especially, since you always help me drive the car."

This retort blew her innate tendency to indulge in back-seat driving into smithereens. She realised why I had interfered in her fields of activity. After this psychological cure, my wife has refrained from helping me with her advice while I drive the car. She merely leans back in her seat and keeps her mouth shut.

Psychological muddle

GETTING out from one muddle, only to find myself caught in some deeper and more complex muddle, is nothing new to me. I have been muddling through life. And I think I will muddle unto death.

What provoked me to think along the lines recorded above needs to be set out clearly. It all began with my introduction to the psychiatrist who has returned from America recently. He assumed that his audience, which included a fairly large sprinkling of married men and aspiring bachelors, apart from widowers, both grass type and the not so grassy type, but no woman, would be delighted to understand the subtle trick which would keep the domestic traingle on the square, which would ensure that the fair sex who ruled the home front did not develop aggressive tendencies. He spelt out his tip. He said that if every man fostered the talent to pep up the spirits of his better half with sweet words, empty compliments and gentle smiles, there would be peace, joy, happiness and cheer all around. With a little diplomacy, the storm at home could be averted.

I was taken in by the cue. I did not realise that I was stepping into trouble. If I could have foreseen the future, I would have given short shrift to the suggestion. But since the future lay shrouded in mystery, since it did not think it proper or necessary to wave the red signal as I decided to try out the panacea offered by the psychologist, I had to wait for the future to unravel itself.

Blissfully ignorant of the trouble in store for me, I returned home, grinning happily. I had a sweet smile, hanging enticingly between my lips, as I was received by my wife. She was surprised to see the smile on my face. Normally, I returned home, after the hectic day in office, with a weary, I-am-tired look, a large scowl on my face, a keep-away-from me sign written large on my mien for my wife to understand.

When she saw the smile on my face, she turned her face wryly. She suspected some deep trouble. She peered at my smile, curled her lips in displeasure and said, "What's the matter with you? You're unusually cheerful. I even see a smile on your face. I hope I am not imagining things."

"Oh, no, dear, there's a smile on my face. And that's not an illusion. I now know that a smile goes a long way in reducing tension. What a formidable weapon is the smile! It stops a quarrel; it brings to an end heated arguments; it soothes a capricious child; it irons out minor creases that soil man-woman relationship. Indeed, a smile sparks off another smile. And with chains of smiles, life becomes strong, happy and durable. So, dear, why don't you smile?"

My wife was not taken in by my words. She stared hard at my smile and commented, "That won't work, not with me, at any rate. That smile on your face gives me the creeps. It is unnatural. And I can suspect many reasons which lie behind that smile."—"And on all the reasons will show you in poor light, will expose you as a man who is ready to violate the code of marital ties, if the chance arises."

"You seem to have a very low estimate of my fidelity."

"Thank God, you get what I mean. Now, drop that smile. Or rather get rid of that childish grin. Change your dress. Wipe your shoes on the doormat before you step in. I don't want all that dirt you have accumulated to be brought in. My house isn't a receptible for all the dirt and filth of Delhi."

I was taken aback by my wife's reaction. I wondered where I had gone wrong. I had only followed the tip of the psychologist who had asserted that a smile disarmed the most aggressive enemy. Yet, it had failed to create any favourable response in my wife.

I slumped on the sofa, waited for my wife to offer me a cup of coffee. She moved to the kitchen, while I removed my shoes, unbuttoned my shirt and let the cool breeze brush over my hairy chest.

When my wife returned with the hot beverage, I took the cup, surveyed her and then commented. "You look glamorous, dear. I'm glad I've such a lovely dame as my life's partner. You can hold your own against any Eve. Why, even Sharmila Tagore will find it difficult to beat you when it comes to looks."

Those were empty compliments, aimed at cheering my wife. Those words were uttered, hopefully. The tactics had been recommended by the psychologist who is supposed to know the secret layers of the conscious, sub-conscious and ultra-conscious complexes of human beings.

I waited for a pleased coo from my wife.

I got the shock of my life when my wife chortled with rage. I was taken aback. I had, unwittingly, roused her fury. She looked like a towering inferno, a raging tornado.

"What're you up to? Gone potty?" growled my wife.

I covered up my dismay. I put on a soothing smile and remarked, "I only sang in praise of your beauty, only said that you compare favourably with the leading light of the Indian screen, the lady who, because of her marriage, can be called the glamorous tigress of the Indian film world."

"That implies that I too am a tigress, hey?"

"Don't put words into my mouth."

"I amn't. And that isn't necessary. You've too many words in your mouth. But I amn't that big an imbecile as to take your words as sweet compliments. You've only paid me a left-handed compliment."

"Oh, no. I mean all that I said. You do look graceful, attractive, alluring. Give me Sharmila and my wife, and I will stand by my dame."

"Stand by her, but ogle at the beauty?"

"Tut, tut. I mean all that I said."

"Well, a few days back, I might have fallen for that bait. But not now. Only the other day, I was casually turning the pages of an old cine magazine. Then I read the candid admission of the film star. Sharmila says in that magazine that she doesn't consider herself to be beautiful. She says her nose is too long. She has a broken tooth, so she doesn't like to smile. She's short and has to watch her weight."

I gaped at my wife in silence. I had no words to counter her. By comparing her to Sharmila Tagore, I had irritated her, turned her into a tigress!

I cursed myself. Why did I choose Sharmila? I could as well have chosen Hema, Rekha or Zeenat, but I had picked up Sharmila. I would have got away with it if only my wife had not by accident rummaged the old magazine and read the confession of the film star that she doesn't think that she is very beautiful, that she could do well with some improvements in her figure.

My wife fumed. I did not speak. I did not want to add fuel to fire by countering her fiery words. The fire raged for an hour, then it subsided.

I have now taken a pledge. I will never try out half-baked ideas spun out by any man, even by a psychiatrist or a psychologist. They don't work. Not with my Eve!

Don't ask for the moon

My wife and I return home after a shopping spree.

I drop the heavy bundle on the sofa, sink into the cushioned seat and sigh in relief. My wife wipes the beads of perspiration with the tip of her sari; before giving me a stern look. I do not notice the sternness in her look till she nudges me and tells, "I never thought you would be so fickle-minded".

"What do you mean? "I sit up, unsure of whether I heard her right. "Don't try to pose as if you are a paragon of virtues. I am rather upset. I never thought you would stare at young girls, who were at the shopping complex, till you lost sight of one to concentrate on another," says my wife.

"But, this is a monstrous charge," I grumble.

"Truth hurts, when it is brought home to you. It hurts me to think that you could behave so callously. We have been married, now, for two decades. And here you are, still ogling at young girls, women young enough to be your daughters," points out my wife.

"Daughters, I have only one. And that one is enough for us..." I try to ward off the discussion.

"You did," my wife insists. Then I recollect how I had noticed a couple of immensely attractive women. Their gait was graceful. Their figures were exotic. And I had stood and watched them with admiration. Beauty, I think, is to be admired. I also have heard that if a man passes a really beautiful woman, without even casting a sly glance at her, the woman feels insulted.

"I plead guilty, dear. But, I did not covet them. I looked at them with sheer admiration. For two of the dames whom we ran into in the shopping complex were immensely beautiful. One of them looked very vibrant and attractive, very much like Vyjayantimala, in her youth. The other one reminded me of Madhubala. They were immensely beautiful and I did appreciate them and look at them," I frankly tell my wife. "So, you don't find me attractive enough," I hear a hurt tone in her voice.

"What gave you the idea? There are attractive women... thousands of them, but, in life, you have to have one girl. She is your own. You are mine, dear. And for me, you are Apsara, Menaka, Cleopatra .... But, that doesn't mean that I shall not look at say, Madhuri Dixit with admiration... And then darling..." I coo. "What then..." My wife is slightly mollified. "One must have an eye for beauty. I admire a lovely rose. I stand and watch with bated breath a cataract on which the sun's rays get refracted. I lose myself to the grand sight of sunrise at Darjeeling. These are nature's gift to man. And I take every chance to enjoy beauty. But, remember, there is no undercurrent of comparison, when it comes down to you and the other girls. You must understand that, dear. For I don't have the advantage that Adam had," I rouse her interest with the last note.

"What is that?"

"The only man, in all creation who never looked at another woman, except his wife, with admiration, was Adam. So don't ask for the moon," I point out, convincing my wife that my interest in the lovely dames means no threat to our marriage.

◆◆◆

All 'keyed' up!

The key to a smooth, unruffled existence, I have been told, lies in maintaining some modicum of order and system in one's style of living. It is personal discipline, advises a book on success... (These days, one observes a plethora of books on the subject by people who have finally found how easy it is to succeed by writing fat tomes on the subject. They are aware of the army of suckers, all over the globe, who assume that they have only to be taught the art of success before they scale the giddy heights of fame. They never see through the game. In most cases, these tomes are actually the means of success for their authors. These suckers may sit, burn the midnight oil, plough their way through the tips, again and again, without ever even getting any wiser on "how to succeed".)...that paves the road to success.

But, the problem which I now face is a bunch of missing keys, which neatly put together and held by a key ring, is nowhere to be found. I have searched...everywhere!

The cupboard has been turned upside down. The whole area, surrounding it resembles a mini battlefield. Myriads of items of all shapes and sizes are strewn around, some of them long lost and given up as untraceable. There is a bank receipt which I had greatly needed to claim back the amount, three years back. I could not find it, then. And I had to wade through a plethora of court affidavits, assurances, guarantees, etc., before I could lay my hands on the amount. Then there is the driving licence, which I had lost, two years back, for which I had finally to procure a duplicate. There are quite a few other documents, papers and things which had managed to lie low when I had hunted them.

The fault may lie with me. I am not the sort of hunter, someone like Jim Corbett, who never gives up the chase till the quarry is laid to rest. I start off with a flourish, but soon my interest wanes. I yawn, throw up my hands in distress, find all sorts of reasons to relax, invite assistance from my wife and children who, all together, create a bigger mess, while the one object I want to track down somehow manages to escape discovery. Rightly has it been said that too many cooks spoil the broth. But to return to the bunch of keys, which I need urgently, so that I can use the car, is missing. I call my family. I instruct them to carry on the search. My son ducks under the bed. My daughter rummages the study. My wife has her run of the kitchen. I relax, now that the army is doing exactly what I had started. My attitude is one of relaxation. I am the boss, here, though I won't state that openly, lest my wife, a dame with a high sense of self-respect, who has never gone beyond a sort of collective leadership, ticks me off for being such a blatant MCP.

Soon, each one of them comes back. The keys are nowhere to be found. I look dejected. My wife starts telling me that this is not the first time I have set the house on fire by asking everyone to look out for something I had misplaced. She hints that 'order' and 'I' are poles apart. There is much truth in what she says, so I can't even use the prerogative of the Speaker who can call several motions out of order. I turn my mind to other topics... The theme for a skit, where I can describe the terrible upheaval at home, over the missing bunch of keys.

Then comes the maid—rattling the keys whose jangling falls like sweet music on my ears—saying she found it in the pocket of the trousers, I had dumped in the laundry basket!

◆◆◆

Riding the storm

I have no inkling of the storm that is brewing up at home, when I drive back, after a tiring day at the office, eager to be in the company of my wife.

My heart misses a beat when I find that my wife is not at the gate, as is her wont. Where has she gone? Why is she not at the gate, with that I-am-glad-you-are-back look in her eyes, a big smile that stretches from ear to ear, leaving no room for any doubt about the delight which suffuses her? My eyebrows rise quizzically as the unexpected absence of my wife at the allotted spot, when I return home, rouses my fears.

I park the car at the gate, swing the gate open, with a bang. I run in shouting, "Hi... Where are you? Not well?"

The front door is open. So, I have no problem in getting in. I call out, once again, "Hi dear... Where are you?"

Silence greets me.

This silence plays havoc with my mental attitude. Where is my wife? Why is she not responding to my call?

I walk, rather stridently, through the drawing room. I push the door of the bedroom, peep in. I spot my wife, lying in the bed, her face buried in the pillow.

"What is the problem, dear?" I get close, bend down and touch her face, gently.

She bounces up, like an enraged tigress.

"Keep away," she shoos me.

"But, why? What have I done to merit such a treatment?" I ask, while sitting by her side.

She sits bolt up, draws away from me, her face red and swollen.

"Anything wrong," I ask.

"Everything," she hisses, angrily.

"Ah. . . That doesn't make sense. You did not indicate any signs of distress, when you saw me off in the morning," I mumble.

"Because the cause for irritation came only now," my wife says between sobs.

"Tell me, and I shall remove that cause in no time."

"Now it is too late," she says.

"Better late than never," I smile at her, but the smile freezes on my face when I notice the icy chill which cloaks her face.

"You seem to be absolutely furious," I try to make some light comment.

"That, I am," she says.

"But, why"?

"You ought to know," says my wife.

"Sorry, dear. You are angry, I am late. Well, I am late by about an hour because the team of auditors from the head office are here. They were grilling me, all day, with questions. They are sniffer dogs. They sniff out every papered-up flaw in the accounts. They have an instinctive knack for that. And they gave me hell the whole of today," I play up my agony, hoping to strike a sympathetic chord in my wife.

"Serves you right," she says, showing no sign of

compassion.

"That is cruel, dear ...I work so hard only to keep the two of us in comfort. And you casually ignore the troubles I take," I indicate my pain.

"You deserved it, fully. Don't you know that today is...." She pauses, looks at me before continuing. "Today is my birthday..," my wife drops the news, making me realise how I had given her cause for pain. I have not only come late, but come without a gift for the occasion. I rue my mistake. Then I search for a way out of the tangle, a means of riding the storm. I spot it, draw my wife closer and please her with the words, "But, dear, you don't look a year older."

"I am thinking of acquiring a Dutch wife," I tell my wife on a sunny morning in September.

"Come September and your senses go berserk," snipes my wife, curling her lips in utter displeasure, indicating her anger at my intention.

"I said I propose to get a Dutch wife," I reiterate indicating my determination to go ahead with my scheme, come what may.

"First things first. You have a wife, so why go in for another one?" My wife assumes a rather soothing tone, assuming that she shall adopt logic to steer me away from the dangerous idea, I am courting.

"Because I can afford a Dutch wife," I respond.

"It does not make sense. You are an Indian. You have married me. In India, for a Hindu, polygamy is a crime. So, even if you import a Dutch wife from across the high seas, you will find yourself in the clutches of the law. I shall set the hounds who maintain the law on your trail. They shall bring you to book, along with your new-found Dutch wife," my wife sounds definitely angry now.

"That is why I have decided to take a Dutch wife. I know I run real danger if I take an English wife or a French wife. I am not keen to get a wife from Malaya or Indonesia or Japan. I shall go in only for a Dutch wife. No power on earth can stop me from getting myself a Dutch wife," I stand my ground.

"My God! What has come over you? Don't you love me?" my wife asks.

"I do. I love you passionately," I mumble.

"Have I failed to satisfy you in anyway? I serve you all the time. I prepare dishes you like. I clean your clothes, iron them, bring them to you when you are getting ready for office. I keep the house spic and span. So, why have you suddenly got it into your head that you must have a Dutch wife? At any rate, I shall not have another woman in this house. That much is certain," my wife is now caught between angry snorts and depressive sobs.

"Now, you don't get me. You are my beloved wife. But, you can never do what the Dutch wife can do," I still speak enigmatically.

"My God! So I have failed you. That makes me feel as if I have lived a worthless life. In what way, can the Dutch wife serve you better than me? And, then, why should a Dutch woman think of marrying a middle-aged, balding, not-too-smart man of fifty?" my wife finds a ray of hope.

"I am not going to seek an answer from the Dutch wife to know whether the latter likes me. I have decided, my dear. I will get myself a Dutch wife. I thought I should take you into confidence before I bring the Dutch wife," I ramble.

"I will tell your mother. She alone can drive sense into your thick head," my wife cries, burying her face in the tip of her *sari*.

"But, there is no need for you to cry. Afterall, I am only getting a Dutch wife," I remonstrate.

"Get out of my sight. I shall have nothing to do with you, until you drop this idea of having a Dutch wife," my wife glares.

"But, dear, a Dutch wife is nothing but an open frame of rattan or cane, used in the East Indies, to rest the limbs upon", I clarify and my wife sees how she has been teased by her man, yet finds enough sunshine to come over and tells me how happy she is to have a husband who prefers a Dutch wife, as his mistress, while many other men go out to find extramarital pleasures.

Believe it or not, we, in this household, are perfectly at home with flying missiles. It is my belief that flying missiles, too, are satisfied with our company. Nay, they feel happy to be at home with a family where every member, from the head of the family (that stands for me, but this is one head which does not enjoy absolute authority and so cannot claim under all circumstances to be the master of the house too), down to the seven-year-old girl in pigtails, finds instant communion with flying missiles and takes to them with alacrity.

Here, for sure, the flying missiles are not stored or put away or stacked for possible use if and when the need arises. That explains why flying missiles seem to revel in this household. They are given enough scope to stay active. If at all the flying missiles in this home may have a complaint, it may be that they are given very little time to rest.

The use of missiles start right from the time the children wake up. The three of them hurl pillows at each other, using the soft cushions, meant to provide support for the necks and the heads, as flying missiles. This pillow war continues unabated, till I walk in and remind them that it is time for them to get ready for school. Reluctantly, they put the pillows back and jump out of bed.

Then begins the hurtling in space of other objects—the tooth paste tube flies from the eldest boy to the next one, before it gets grabbed by the girl with the pig tails. The first one gets hold of the tooth brushes, instantly recognises them as flying missiles and gives a chance to his two siblings to perfect the fine art of tracking down flying objects or eluding their range or grabbing them with confidence. Clothes fly around. Books hurtle through space. Pens and pencils turn into darts. Even tiffin boxes, which are empty, have their flying trajectory, despite the fact that often enough, the two or more parts of the boxes decide they would rather spin separately, creating a lot of confusion.

The fault does not lie with the children. They have learnt the art, I am sure, from their parents.

I still love to tell my wife how much I love her by sneeking in from behind, hurling a scented rose at her, using the flower as a flying missile, deftly sending it into space so that it strikes her rosy cheek. She, in turn, grabs a jasmine tucked in her *veni*, and gets a direct hit by turning it into a flying missile.

My wife uses the paper dart to bring me out of the spell cast by the crossword puzzle in the newspaper. She rolls up a sheet of paper, makes a paper ball and hits me with it when she thinks I am not listening to what she is saying. Sometimes, many things in the kitchen, which are brought in to aid the culinary art, turn into flying objects.

When I lose my temper, I let books fly in all directions. Or, I hurl pens and pencils all around though I avoid aiming them at anyone in particular. The few hits I have made have been more accidental than intentional. However, this is immaterial. The message is clear. If there is a home where the flying missiles are perfectly at home, that, beyond doubt, is my own home.

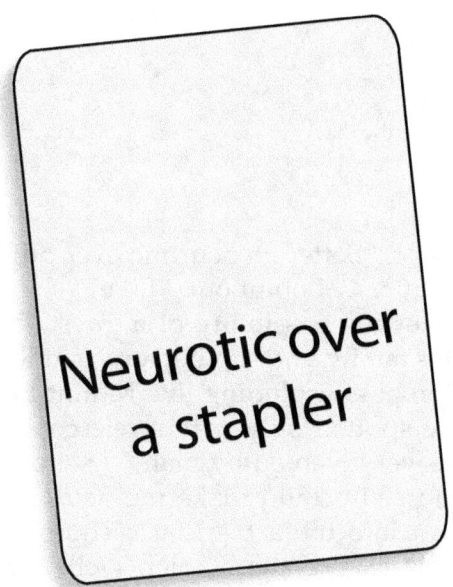

Neurotic over a stapler

I swing high with the bright idea of acting the role of a normally sane man who quite unexpectedly gets frightened by an innocuous modern contraption around the house. I look around for such an object. The stapler, the small and compact instrument that clips and binds sheets, in the proper order, or seals the slits of envelope with wide open mouths that need to be sealed, comes in handy. I pick up the stapler, turn it around in my hand and wait to begin the act. I don't want to play-act to an empty house. That, I know, is senseless. So I wait till my wife walks into the study and starts the grand show. I scream, producing eerie notes that chill the bravest of the brave and hurl the stapler with all the force at my command, out into space. It races through the air, hits the wall with a thud and drops to the floor. I stare at the fallen object and then laugh hysterically. "Hi, what has come over you?" my wife rushes to my side and forces me to lock glances with her. "That accursed object, the stapler, gives me a real scare," I speak with a quiver in my voice. "I won't have it anywhere around. It must go. It is the stapler or me in this house. Make your choice, lady, quickly," my voice trembles. "Have you gone mad?" my wife can't believe her ears. "The stapler is driving me mad," I admit. "You, a man, scared of a stapler!" she snarls. "Doesn't a man have a right to have his fears?" I work up, with some amount of skill, quite a tremor.

"You are getting neurotic over piffle," says my wife while I gape, with assumed fear-stricken eyes, at the stapler on the floor. "Better go neurotic over piffle than over more serious matters," I point out. "Like?" she asks. "Like getting scared over the possibility of a guest, landing at our place, with his family, and staying for extended periods! Like imagining the boss exploding like Mount Etna over an error that can be spotted only with a telescope more powerful than any as yet invented by man," I set down a variety of fears that possibly could make me neurotic, but haven't, mercifully, got into the act, so far. "Those fears are unexceptionable. But fear of the stapler, well, it is inane," my wife can't believe herself. "I know. But suppose someone produces a giant stapler that pins the employee at his desk as soon as he reports for work! Suppose this pin is removed only after he has finished the day's job! Where will that leave me? Imagine a stapler that can seal our mouths and silence us! How then shall we eat! Shall we die of starvation?" I let my imagination fly high. "You and your silly notions!" my wife realises that I am play acting, picks up the stapler and places it on the table. "So you have made your choice! You can live with the stapler. I leave, right away," I make a mock show of bowing out, before joining my wife in rings of laughter that eddy around the room.

Potshots at Oneself

If anybody, who is not moulded in the traditional format of a hero, is an anti-hero, I can claim to be just that. (There may be pundits who may snivel, saying that an anti-hero should be one who is all out to bring the hero down on his heels. They may say that either one is a hero or one is not a hero. But not being a hero does not make one an anti-hero. These armchair critics are not going to put me down.) I am an anti-hero because everything that I am flies against the nature and character of the hero. Is that not proof enough that I am one of the anti-heroes around, in our vast country?

The realisation that I am not a hero does not leave me down and out. On the contrary, the awareness has saved me from many an ugly situation.

Every time opportunity knocks, (that is one thing that opportunity does, with unfailing regularity and insistence), inviting me to play the role of the hero, I have deliberately cold-shouldered the invitation. I have refused to be taken in by the glory that will be mine, if only I get into the act. I never let myself be inveigled by such invitations for, I do not wear glasses.. coloured glasses.. when I look at myself.

So, when an eveteaser decides to have some fun, at the expense of a young girl, in the bus, I turn to anyone close to me, sturdy and strong enough, to step in and be the hero. I always manage to find someone who is willing to be a hero. There is no paucity of heroes in our society.

When the man I choose for the role succeeds in driving sense into the hooligan, I cheer. I cheer vociferously. I shake his hands, warmly. I hail him as a hero. I compliment him for his valour. I praise him, skyhigh, for being so gallant, a view with which the girl, now regaining her poise after the unpalatable experience, quickly agrees.

It is the same in other situations, too.

I inspire others around to be heroes. I have inspired a person to nab a pickpocket. I have acted as a catalyst in egging a neighbour to protest against the casual attitude of some of the municipal employee, who dumped *malba* across the road, where our houses stand. I have screamed and shouted in appreciation, every time someone or the other played the hero in real life, often proving the prowess which carries shades of the superhuman survival capacity shown by heroes on the silver screen.

Without the slightest grudge, I have cheered the hero. The realisation that I have nothing of the hero in me, that I am a perfect anti-hero, makes it easy for me to be the leader of the cheer gang. Rightly did the wag quip, "We can't all be heroes. Somebody has to be there to clap and cheer and applaud the heroes".

Heroes of the world, listen! You have a readymade fan who shall sing your praise, without any reservation. Befriend me, the anti-hero, and people like me. We are the exact opposite of the hero. So, our mutual attraction stays strong. For, the scientist says, 'Opposites attract each other'.

Buttoned out

The time the button chooses to part itself from the shirt and drop off is invariably most inopportune. One moment, my fingers are holding it firmly in place. I struggle to force the button, which sticks to the lower lapel, through a tiny vertical slit in the upper lapel and then shall the button perform its duty, happily. Can any duty be easier to perform? The button is assigned the task of keeping flaps, that usually stay apart, together. This task is neither strenuous nor tiring. Moreover, it has its pleasures too. The button rules it high over the flaps. I wonder whether the button teases the flaps, saying, "You are my prisoners. I have brought you together. You stay united, whether you like each other or not, till I set you free," forgetting the fact that it is a prisoner held in bondage by the lower flap by fine thread that runs in and out through the holes of the button. I enjoy this train of thought, while trying to get the button through the slit. I am blissfully unaware of the fact that repeated visits by the shirt to the washing machine has weakened the thread that binds the button to the lapel, that the tenuous hold of the lapel on the button is weaker than the *kamzor kadi*, about which much may be said by Neena Gupta. The force I use to get the button in place is the final snip. The thread snaps, instantly the button drops off, hits the ground, rolls fast, slips under the bottom of the bookcase and vanishes from sight. It takes me a second to realise the immensity of the tragedy. I have hardly a minute or two to get dressed and hurry over to the bus stop to catch the chartered bus.

A minute is an expanse of time when it comes to getting a button through a slit, but it is too short a time to track down the errant button, bind it back on the lower lapel and order it to get back to duty. Nor is one minute enough to find a new button that matches the four other buttons that are dutifully performing their task from a plastic container that is a storehouse of an assortment of buttons and stitch it in place... So I quickly unbutton the bonds of the lapels, take the shirt off, dump it and reach out for another shirt. It has two buttons missing. Another shirt has the buttons in place, but one of the buttons presents a burnt look, having been scalded by the heat of the iron, carelessly dragged over it. The fourth shirt I pick up doesn't match the shade of the pants I wear. But I have no more time to seek out yet another shirt. Dishevelled, dressed in shirt and pants that don't match, I hurry to the bus stop, run to catch the handle of the entrance of the bus, that is slowly picking up speed and haul myself in with a firm kick on the ground. In the process, the button of the cuff of the right sleeve breaks away and seeks company with the dust and dirt while I bemoan my fate. Then the thought surfaces once again. The time the button chooses to part itself from the shirt and drop off is invariably the most inopportune.

The impossible, or rather the near impossible, has happened.

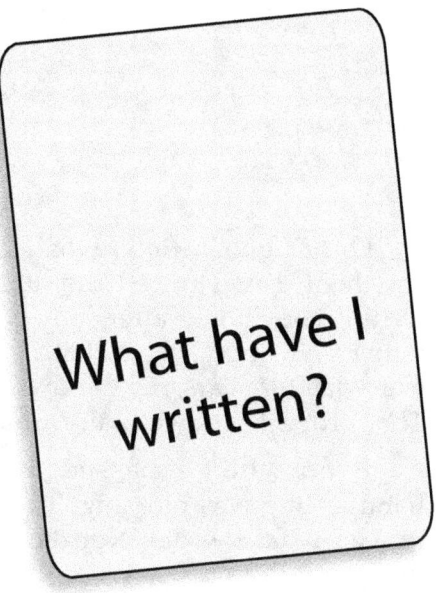

I have a note, written by me. And I can't make head or tail of it. I can't decipher it. It is more complex and testing than even the Indus Valley script.

I had written a note to my wife a month back, while she was away at her parent's place. She had failed to understand what I had to say. Now, on her return, she has given it to me. She wants me to tell her what I have written.

Her demand sends a chill through me. For I feel, instinctively, that my handwriting may be beyond me to read.

This is no empty premonition. I hold the note in my hand. I turn it, hold it close to my eyes, examine it from all angles. But I fail to make any sense of it. The writing is absolutely illegible. There is no way I can dig out the message concealed in the scribbling. I may do penance for a hundred years, carry out research with the help of a computer and an army of men, yet, I know, for certain, that I will not land on the contents of the note.

"Come on, dear. You must be able to read your own handwriting," my wife eggs me on.

"I should be, but I can't," I throw up my hands in utter disgust.

"Well, if even you can't read your handwriting, how can I?" she mumbles and moves off.

I wonder how it happened.

Once upon a time, I had a fairly good hand. While at school, I had traced the alphabets hundreds of times, writing copy books after copy books. I was then told by my father and my teachers that if I wrote two pages of copy everyday for years, my handwriting will become neatly set. That order, I followed, all through my middle school.

Even when I passed out of the university, my handwriting was pleasing. There was no difficulty for me to read what I wrote. Nor did my friends complain about my handwriting.

The deterioration, I now realise, began after I stopped writing. I began to type things out on a battered old machine at home. At office, I always have a steno to take dictation.

Slowly, writing became something alien to my nature. Gradually, a stage came when I picked up the pen only when I had to sign.

No wonder my handwriting has become so rotten that even I can't read it.

"Still musing on your undecipherable note?" my wife comes in with a cup of coffee. I put the note aside, pick up the cup of coffee and grumble, "I never knew my handwriting has gone to the dogs."

"Wrong, my dear," laughs my wife and adds, "Even dogs won't touch your handwriting with the longest of long poles."

I take the snipe in good spirits. There is nothing else I can do.

I have achieved virtually what is considered impossible. I have developed a handwriting which none can read. Not even I.

◆◆◆

Waterloo

Nobody can say that I am a nincompoop, yet I invariably end up as one when I find myself forced into a fight with anything that comes under the generic name, Package. Take, for example, the new inland letter that is fashioned on the pattern of the foreign air letter. The new shape is sleek, not squarish all over as before. But that is the only good thing about the new form. Everything else about the three-edged stuck-up demon, as I call it, rouses my ire. The worst irritants of the new format are its three sealed edges. The moment such a letter comes in by the post, I lose my cool. I imagine the air resonating with the jeering notes of letter, "I will show this man for what he is, a fool who cannot unwrap me neatly so that he could get the message I carry. He totally lacks the basic skill needed to handle packages, whatever be their shape or size." Those words make me mad, blind my common sense. I resolve, then and there, to cut through the edges, unfold the letter and read the contents and thus, prove to the world at large that I am not such a dullard when it comes to getting into the contents of a sealed inland letter. I place the inland letter on the table, hold a blade, carefully, between the thumb and the index finger, examine the edges with the eye of a trained surgeon, decide where I shall make the first cut and tell myself that I shall cut into the heart of the letter. Instantly, pride suffuses me. The pride has its roots in the realisation that I have much in common with Christian Barnard, the man who carried out the first heart transplant.

A supercilious smile dances between my lips when the blade cuts through one edge; then the second and finally the third. Quickly I put the blade back where it belongs, lift the letter and try to unfold it. Then I get a real shock. The order of the contents of the letter is in total disarray. The beginning has turned into the middle; the middle has gone to the end; and the end to the beginning. Everything is topsy turvy. I imagine, then, the letter clapping its hands, shouting, while it takes its last breath, if it has one, "Lo and behold! The world's greatest incompetent package opener!" Quietly, I shove the letter aside and sulk. My daughter walks in and works wonders. My sulk vanishes in a trice. "*Papa*," she holds out a little plastic ketchup package that is slick and slippery, and says, "Please open it, *papa*. I failed." I think this task is easy. The package is supposed to be easy to tear open with one's fingers. So I pick it up, try to tear it open with the force of my fingers, but the sealed top fails to open up. I decide, then, to tear the edge off with my teeth. This time, the edge rips open, before I am ready to take my teeth off. I get a mouthful of ketchup, while the rest of it drips on to the front of my shirt. What my daughter sights are an empty package and a father who has ketchup on his lips and all over his dress. Now you know that when it comes to packages, the farther I am from them, the better it is for me.

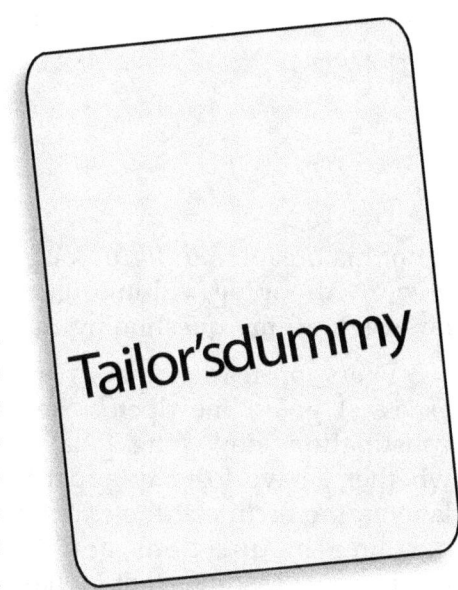

Tailor's dummy

In my chequered existence on this planet for more than five decades, I have run into a large number of tailors and drapers. I have gone, back and forth, from one to another, very much in the manner of a football that gets kicked around on the field, trying to spot the one tailor who would somehow manage to match my body to the clothes he makes for me. But such a tailor, if he exists, has managed to give me the slip.

I have a nagging suspicion somewhere at the back of my mind that the fault lies with me. I am endowed with some rare quality which defies the best efforts of tailors. This quality somehow makes it impossible for the tailor to make clothes which fit me to the T.

The tailor assumes, automatically, that he will run into no problems when he decides to accept my costume. He feels confident he will do a good job. His measuring tape hugs me, runs over me, forms a loop around my neck, encircles my waist, tightens round the thighs, while he feverishly jots the readings on his pad. He makes me turn and twist. He raps me for stooping. He pulls me up for wriggling when he touches ticklish spots.

Then he begins to grill me. Do I need a back pocket for the trousers? How wide or narrow should the lowest extremities be? Do I like my clothes skin-tight? Or do I prefer them baggy?

These queries make me wild. If I am to tell the tailor how he should go about his task, what is he there for? Is it not his business to figure out what sort of tailoring will give my drooping, wilting figure the right image? Why is he wasting time questioning me?

Every professional does this kind of questioning to excess. I go to the doctor; he asks me whether I have constipation, how long I have been feeling run down, whether I have lost my appetite. It is the same with the lawyer, the architect, the tax consultant. I have withstood barrages of questions and learnt one lesson. Every professional assumes that he has a right to grill his clients. But such questions do not necessarily help him give the client better service.

I still recollect the time I went to a dentist, answered a lot of questions, as his torture instrument tip-toed over my teeth like a ballerina. Finally, catching the wince and the cry of pain and identifying the tooth which was bothering me, he gave me something to apply and asked me to return once the pain had subsided. And then, you guessed it, he pulled out the healthy tooth, and the one that had caused pain stayed put. So much for the efficacy of questions by professionals.

The tailor assures me that he will have the clothes ready soon enough. I enquire about the fit. He says he has never failed a customer.

But, when the pants strangle the waist and the shirt collar can accommodate half a neck more, I go back to him, only to be told, after much hedging, that I have a body which no tailor, even the best at Saville Row, can drape. I remain the tailor's challenge.

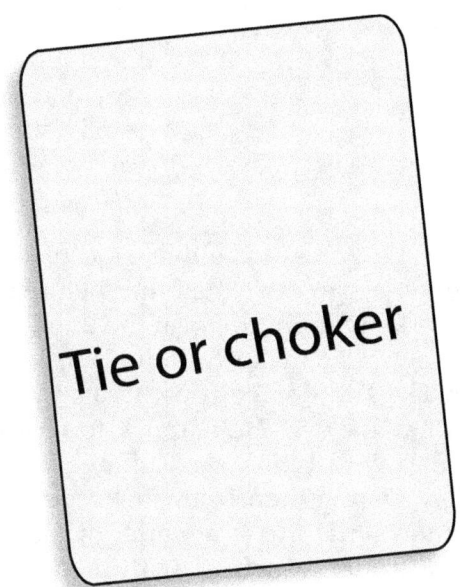

Can anything shatter the confidence of a young man, from a remote small town, than the need to readjust to life in a big metropolis? Specially for one, who has never tried his hand at bringing the button and the buttonhole of the collar together, tying a knot of the tie and pulling the lower flap till the knot gets to the neck, stopping short of further tug that shall make it difficult for him to breathe freely?

This is the problem a callow young man, straight-talking, untrained in the ways of sham postures and false facades, from regions, viewed as outlandish and untouched by civilisation by the people of big cities, faces when he is transported, by the need to seek a living to a metropolis. He is told, when he reports for duty, in a shirt that bares the neck and exposes the Adam's apple and gives it full freedom to present itself in all its bare glory, that he is improperly dressed.

"What is wrong with my dress?" he asks with a straight face. "You are not sporting a tie, young man," the senior grunts. "A tie is a must for all male employees." The young man nods his head.

In the evening, he buys a couple of ties on the way back to his room from the office and seeks help from a friend on how to tie the knot.

The friend demonstrates how to prepare a single knot, how to work with a double knot. He prepares the knots, while explaining each step... how to adjust the ends while the tie hangs on either side of one's neck, how to make one flap go over the other before the ends are twisted and worked around to form the knot, how to pull the lower end down and make the knot move up to tighten round the neck. The novice tries his hand. His friend watches with a hawk's eye. He is quick to reprimand, ready to rap and snap with biting sarcasm every time the novice blunders. The young man faces this ordeal, boldly, defiantly. For he knows that this is a matter of life, that his bread and butter are firmly entwined with the tie. He has to learn to wear it; or get ready to join the army of the unemployed. That possibility is enough to steel his will and breathe into him the will to go through the steps a hundred times before he manages a knot that is passable. Then he pulls the lower end rather firmly. The knot moves up and presses round his neck. It leaves him choked, bleary eyed. The trainer intervenes in time and averts what could otherwise have proved fatal. Practice makes perfect. The novice learns to knot the tie properly. He knows instinctively when to stop pulling the lower end, lest it ends up as a real choker.

Well, you may ask how I know the pains of the battle between a novice and a tie? Examine me, carefully, and you will spot, behind my old, weather-beaten frame, the callow youth whose encounter with the tie is the theme note of this skit.

The book that comes in by courier, with a note from the Editor to review the book, lifts my spirits, instantly. I feel like the lark, light and gay, ready to sing any merry tune, however hoarse and untrained my voice be to others, sure that there could be no more soulfilling music than the one I churn out from the depths of my very beings. This music is mine alone to hear and enjoy. It is sweeter than the sweetest of notes that a Sonu Nigam or a Hariharan or a Jagjit Singh could produce. The reason is not far to seek. Each one of us is gifted and has an ear for his/her own music. This inner ear tunes best with the songs one sings to oneself. Others may rubbish the music as cacophony, yet it makes the singer believe that he or she is the greatest musician alive today. I hum a tune, feel immensely happy. My happiness has its roots in the awareness that reviewing the books shall help me keep the wolf out of the door for a few days.

Then comes a fear. It thrives on a quotable quote, held in a state of animated suspense, buried deep in the folds of my grey cells, that suddenly decides that it is time it seizes the limelight. Believe me, even quotable quotes love the halo, which is another name for the limelight. The quote, attributed to the famous novelist, Noel Coward, says, "I love criticism so long as it's unqualified." I am taken aback. It takes me sometime to realise the wisdom that the quote holds. No artist has ever taken criticism that fails to be unqualified praise with equanimity. Almost immediately the criticised becomes the critic. He castigates the reviewer, hits back with a quote. "The man who can does. The man who can't criticise," and hauls the critic over a bed of scalding red hot coal. That is an operational risk that a critic who cannot lie to himself and call every polished stone a *Kohinoor*, faces. Am I ready to face this ordeal? The growl of the wolf, followed by the scraping notes produced by the sharp paws of the animal on the door, provide the answer. By reviewing the books, I shall manage to strengthen my defence against the marauding wolf. That takes priority. I pick up the book, sharpen my critical faculties to needle points and get set to plunge into the task. "One minute," a voice from deep within dishes out some sound advice. "Before you criticise someone, you should walk a mile in their shoes. That way, when you criticise them, you are a mile away from them, and you have their shoes." Put yourself, dear reader, in my shoes, and you will instantly sense why I now have the courage to play the role of a critic.

For whom belloc tolls

Whoever first spoke of 'here now, gone next moment' syndrome must have stumbled on the quotable quote after exposure to the shock caused by the swiftness with which one of the sturdy equipment in his holdings, considered to be incapable of calling it a day, suddenly decided that it had rendered enough service and the time had come for it to turn from activity to total inactivity. One moment, it was pulsating with vim and vigour, if I could say so. Yet, the very next moment it had turned totally dead. Dead like the dodo!

I receive a shock, similar to one endured by the enunciator of the syndrome, when the power socket that had worked perfectly well till yesterday, turns totally inert today. I drive the pins of the plug, at the end of a wire that has its roots in the body of a table fan, into the socket, hoping to receive a waft of cool air. But the fan's blades do not set out on a mad whirl, show no indication to take to the spin. I shake the body of the fan, vigorously, confident that I could somehow stir it into action. But the expected doesn't happen. I go back and check whether the pins of the plug are firmly driven into the socket. The coupling is perfect. But the fan still doesn't work. I pull the plug out, take the fan to the next room and link it with the socket there. And lo presto! the fan throws out gusts of wind with its usual gusto.

Then it strikes me. The socket that I used first to make the fan work has developed some problem. I refuse to believe that it can't be repaired, revived and restored to life. With pursed lips, I walk to the shelf, grab the tool box and get ready for the task. My wife, who keeps a hawk's eye on me, knows, instinctively, when I am swinging high with grandiose ideas that do not mesh well with my native abilities. She decides to warn me, sounds the siren and forces me to back away from the plan before I mess around enough to qualify for the title, 'THE BEST NINCOMPOOP THIS SIDE OF THE SUEZ'. She does that, this time too.

"Call Muthu, the electrician. He knows how to do the job. He shall replace the socket," she says. "But, dear, this is a simple job. I have a spare socket in the tool kit. I see no danger in taking on the task. I shall pull out the fuse, so that the supply of electricity is temporarily suspended," I argue. "Ah, poor dear writer husband! I am sure you will see the wisdom in the words of great writers and refrain from tinkering with the socket," my wife grins. "What do the great writers say?" I growl under my breath.

"Cervantes whispers in your ears the warning, 'My dear Don Quixote, don't tilt at electric sockets. They can be more deadly than windmills!' Your all-time favourite Hilaire Bello warns you not to play the role of Lord Fenchley, sing this requiem, 'Lord Fenchley tried to mend the electric light himself. It struck him dead; and serve him right'. It is the business of the wealthy man/to give employment to the artisan."

She has her way. Muthu replaces the socket and leaves. I don't replace the socket and live to tell the tale.

Is picking pockets such a big crime? Is there one person in this universe, who has not picked pockets ever? The answer is an emphatic NO. A No that has the decibel strength far in excess of what a jet aircraft churns out at take-off or landing.

I pick pockets; and I get away with it. Not only from the police, but also from my own conscience. That's the truth. Nothing but the truth, so God help me.

All very confusing, I agree, till I tell you that I pick ... let me break the suspense... my own pockets. And, that, I think, is no crime.

Why do I do that? Elementary, my dear Watson! I pick pockets because I am a normal human being and love treasure troves as much as every other person. What are pockets of apparels, not worn for long, but treasure troves?

What are the treasures I find? Well, it could be the idea for a skit, casually scribbled on a railway ticket and shoved into the pocket and forgotten for months; or a quotable quote copied from a billboard at a major intersection on the back of a publicity sheet, handed over to me by one of the road-side urchins, and tucked away in a pocket. I can list quite a few other items that go into my pockets... visiting cards, coins and currency notes, even an odd letter or two handed over by the LOH for posting, waiting to reach the mail box.

When do I turn to this dubious role? The right moment, let me tell you, is when the LOH goes off on a shopping spree or to join a kitty party or a *bhajan mandali*, on a Sunday afternoon. Then I get enough time to hunt out the treasures from the pockets of the pants and the shirts and the coats. Not once am I disappointed.

My fingers grope around a crumbled sheet, in one of the coat pockets. It turns out to be a hundred-rupee note. When did I stack it there? How did I forget about it, all these months? I push such questions aside, feel the happiness that comes to a man who is richer by hundred bucks.

After savouring this happiness, I seek more treasures. A few coins spill out. One of them is an old one paisa coin, something which I am told commands today a price of about Rs 10 because it has become an antique item. How foolish of me not to have conserved all the one paise coins, when they were around in abundance? If only I had conserved them, I would be sitting pretty today.

I overcome the pain at the loss I have suffered due to my lack of farsightedness and start picking pockets. I find, apart from a few visiting cards and a few notes on which I had scribbled ideas for development into articles and skits and short stories, a flat stone that I had used, during a visit to the lake, about two months back, where I vied with my nephew, making the stone frog-leap.

Time flies. Does it frog-leap? The buzzer shrieks, makes me frog-leap to the door and open it. My wife who walks in, sniffs the air, spots the clothes strewn around on the floor and jokes, "So the pickpocket was at work."

I confess I pick my own pockets. Pray, tell me, dear reader, whose pockets do you pick?

M̲y image in the mirror gives me a bolt from the blue. Where does the blue, a shade that dyes the sky to present a picture of all-is-well-with-this-world image, a colour that qualifies films to  deny them access to theatres and to force them to the privacy of drawing rooms because of restraints imposed by the code of the censors when it comes to depicting sex, keep the bolt that has made me its target? I try to locate the quiver in which blue holds its bolts. A bolt from the blue, I remember, is an idiom. It stands for an unexpected revelation. How idiotic of me to have tried to locate the bolt in the blue, when this bolt has no tangible existence! I shake free of this feeling of inanity. Instantly, I see the bolt that goes with the blue which stands for an unexpected revelation. I survey the figure that peers at me from behind the mirror. Its hair is as white as snow. Its eyes, sunk, listless, display the stamps of crow's feet below them. Lines on its forehead resemble deep furrows on a recently tilted field. The cheeks are puffed out. The lips are dry and cracked. Everything about the image speaks of old age.

Where from has this image sprung? I pout my lips; and so does the image. I roll my eyes; and the copycat does that too.

I turn away from the mirror, telling myself that there must be something wrong with the mirror. "You said it," says a voice in my head that I identify as that of John T West. My head fills with the words of this song, written by West: "The other day, I happened by chance,/As I passed a mirror, to give it a glance,/And I wondered, who that old man could be,/Who, with his mouth wide open, was looking at me./His bald head was sprinkled with a little grey fuzz. And he wasn't at all handsome (like I always was)./He looked like a sack of mismated parts,/Put together without aid of instructions or charts./And while I know that my shoulders don't slump,/This person's were misshapen in one ugly hump!/Now, if that was my image, I can only say? They don't make mirrors like they did in my day." Aye, Aye! Dear West! In the East too, these days, they don't make mirrors like they did in our days. Come on. Let us track down Kipling and give him the happy tidings that the mirrors of today have made the twain meet.

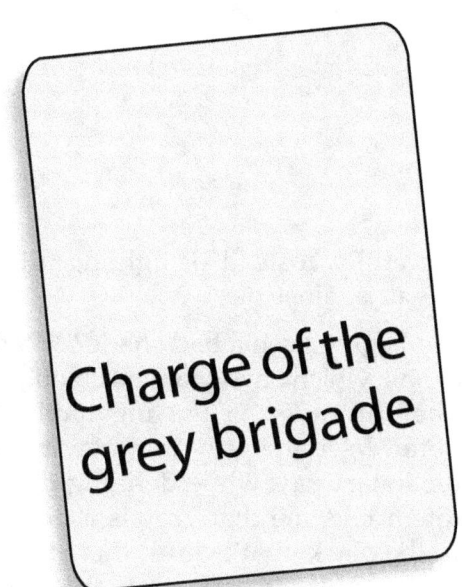

Charge of the grey brigade

How does one react when he sights the first strand of grey hair in the mirror and tries to run the comb through the hair so as to enhance his looks? I think it must be akin to the terrific shock which runs through me, when I notice the greyishness in the sea of black.

I stamp my feet angrily, stomp around like a bear that had an overdose of honey and behave like a rogue elephant. It takes me time to cool down, to regain control over myself. I realise that there is very little that I can do to hold back the march of the *Grey Brigade*. I also sense that the few hair, which get left behind on the comb are all black. Rightly did Daniel Bridegram note, "I have nothing against grey hair. I just wish they were the ones that fell out."

The grey hair stay put, though I run the comb, again and again over the areas where the touch of grey dominates. I hope, foolishly though, that the grey hair, in my case, would react in a different way. But, the grey hair have found their home. They have come home to rest. They want to turn me into a 'grey eminence'. No power on earth can arrest their onward march. They know no Waterloo. They shall win, however strong my resistance. Napoleon had his Elba. *Able was I ere I saw Elba, he cried*. But, the grey hair have no such Elba; so their ability to have their way, remains.

That realisation works wonders with me. I sense that I should learn to live with the new arrivals. I must yield gracefully, instead of fighting a battle with the odds that are all against me.

Is grey such a bad shade? Afterall, I look at the strands of hair, which have changed colour, overnight, with tolerance. The surrender to the inevitable restores my balance of mind. I see the grey in a new perspective. What does the dictionary say, while defining the colour grey? The big fat totem tells me that grey is a deft mix of white and black. In the black, that is grey, there is no element of white. And in the white, that is grey, there is no touch of black. So, how does one define the colour? Is it not elusive like the eel? Is it not as slippery as quick silver?

When it comes to defining greyishness, we are like the seven blind men of Arabia who tried to learn all about the elephant by running their fingers over the pachyderm, limiting their study to the part of the animal which readily came within their teach. Thus, the man who got hold of the tail concluded that the beast was a close cousin of the rope. "No," said the man who had a date with its leg. "It is firm like the pillar." Each one had a different perspective.

I now know that GREY is white, black and all that lies between white and black!

Those who have been sneering at me, for long, because I often present views and concepts which strike against what they consider is logical and sensible, will now have to tone down their critical notes. No longer can they assert that my logic is contorted and convoluted, that when it comes to rhyme and reason, I am as good as a goner, that scan as they may, all around the globe, they shall still fail to see someone so bereft of sense as this scribe. I know how much they shall suffer because the target of their venomous attack, this scribe, has now something to throw back at them, something that leaves them no more room to snipe at. At last, the scientists have thrown in their weight and started singing the praise of the fuzzy logic.

Nearly thirty years back, Lotfi Zadeh, an American mathematician, put across the theory of fuzzy logic. He argued that there are so many imponderables, in every situation, that trying to get to the root of the problem, only through logic, shall often leave one deeper in a mess. The sniggers and the sneezers refused to accept his statement. They crowned him as the king of the blockheads, found enough logic to raise hell for him because he advocated a cause which failed to appeal to those who dressed themselves up in straitjackets. Logic, which remains, even today, their coat of arms, breathed strength into them when they tried to cut down Zadeh for being in the right with the fuzzy logic.

Now their logic has struck a bad patch. For, in real life, we run into problems, every now and then. Every problem demands individual attention. Merely trying to tackle it, on the basis of predefined logical assumptions, shall often lead us into deeper mess. I, for one, have been ardently dating fuzzy logic, since the time I realised that my grey cells always work at cross purposes, that I have too many of them, endowed with the touch of individuality, that each one of them follows a line of logic which is at variance with the reasoning of its neighbour. My grey cells do not believe in peaceful co-existence with their neighbours. They are ready to go at each other's jugulars, show no restraint when they claw at each other, indicate that they shall defend their ideas and ideals even if it means annihilation. The confusion they churn out is truly befuddling. And, all that I do when the grey cells fight it out among themselves, is to remain a passive spectator. I do not try to order them around, (as a Napoloen or a Cariappa or a Zia would do), force them to fall in line. My ability to discipline the grey cells is next to nothing.

I used to think, every time my friends had hearty laughs because I presented my fuzzy logic, how much better off I would be if only I could learn to be as precise, calculating and as exact as them. But, now, I know, thanks to Zadeh and his fuzzy logic, which today is the most potent weapon in the armoury of electronic industry, that I am in the right with one or two, that I can now commend myself for being so loyal and bold in my adherence to the weird, contorted, illogical fuzzy logic.

Defending poor memory

Light chooses its own time to land on areas of ignorance. It is nobody's handmaid. Therein lies the power and the excitement which light holds.

How did the realisation that the earth exerts a pull on every object within reach come to Sir Isaac Newton? It came to him out of the blue. It knocked him on the head, with vicious power. We can imagine poor Newton, rubbing the bump on his head, wondering why he had been hit. After all, he had done nobody any harm. Yet, he was at fault. He had assumed that the apple tree was free from malice. The shade of the apple tree seemed to him the right royal place to sit and let his thoughts wander. He did not know that there was an apple, ripe and ready to cut the umbilical cord that tied it to the tree and to find its way through life.

All that it wanted was a suitable landing site. Newton's head provided just that. The apple freed itself from the clutches of the tree and came down on Newton's head. That was how Newton saw light. That light made him famous. He discovered gravity. Everyone hailed him as a genius. Nobody noticed his mental blockades.

On one occasion, he invited a friend for dinner. The friend arrived in time for the appointment. Newton was immersed in research. Time sped by. The guest told the housemaid that he was feeling hungry. "Go and tell your master that I am here," he told her. She suggested, "Sir, you take your dinner. Mr Newton will not mind. You know him. When he works, he forgets all else."

The guest knew she was right. He had his dinner. Sometime later, Newton emerged from his study. He groaned, "I am awfully hungry," His eyes riveted on the plate, on which lay remnants of food. Then he told himself, "So, I have had my dinner." The housemaid and the guest told him that he had not had his dinner. They explained. Newton laughed, owned up his absent-mindedness.

If Newton could be absent-minded, why can't I be? That is the defence I provide when friends charge me of poor memory. Initially, their charge used to hurt me. I used to tell them, "One swallow doesn't a summer make. Nor one incident of poor memory a forgetful man make."

But, when my forgetfulness became the talk of the town, (That's an idiom. The town did not go about publishing my forgetfulness), I sensed the futility of trying to cover up the truth. Now, I have become immune to the charge. When someone tells me I am absent-minded, I tell my critic, "That puts me in august company." The listener looks foxed. He can't for the life of him, make out how I could be proud of my absent-mindedness.

Then I tell him, "Do you know that Newton was absent-minded?" Before he reacts, I roll out the anecdote from Newton's life.

I pepper it with the story of G. K. Chesterton. Once, he lost his way in a London suburb. He wired home, "Where am I"

I have a rich collection of stories about the forgetfulness of eminent people. I quote a few and then ask my friend, "I know I have memory lapse. Who doesn't have? I am in the company of celebrities when I am absent-minded!"

A form of inspiration

I AM not against hard work, at all. In fact, I fully endorse the call, sent out periodically by our leaders, that the nation can progress only if the people put in hard work. I know that success is 99 per cent perspiration and one per cent inspiration. Work, the dictum says, should be worship. I hold nothing against this dictum, either. I don't grudge, so long as everyone is asked to put in hard work. Including me.

I do not hate the work period.

In fact, I have my work cut out for me. I love to sit before the typewriter, to insert a clean white sheet of paper on the roller and then gape at the ceiling. Many people, who catch me, idly gaping at the ceiling, or scratching my pate or nibbling a biscuit, left on a plate by my wife who knows that I am the breadwinner and that, I can be a breadwinner only if I have my energy pack well charged, or sipping slowly the cup of coffee which turns from steaming hot to hot, to tepid to cold by the time, I empty the cup and finish the last drop of the magic potion, rush to the conclusion that I am good at putting on a big show about hard work. They say that I do not burn calories while I work.

Even white-collar workers, which include officers too, at least, walk from one room to another, carrying files; or they discuss burning much energy in verbal, arguments and pleas and encounters; or they lift files, piles of them, bringing them out of the almirahs in the morning and putting them back in the almirahs in the evening.

I do nothing of the sort. I sit, my eyes glazed, my gaze riveted somewhere on the ceiling, while my fingers which ought to be tapping merrily on the keyboard, have all the rest they need. This posture gives people the impression that work and I are poles apart.

That is the tragedy of my profession.

I am a writer. I have to whip up my grey cells into a real ferment. Only then do they come to grips with the subject which is at the core of the thought processes. It takes time for the mind to grapple with diverse facts. It needs quite a lot of facts, stored in the memory, to be dug out.

The mind is a computer, though often enough, the mind takes more time to dig out the required information. But, the brain holds an edge over the computer, as far as mine is concerned. It works, even though superficially, it looks as if I am doing nothing. The brain, in a way, is where all the hard work goes on, where the ideas to go into an article are properly analysed, where unwanted details are spiked, where the text is prepared, revised, remodelled and finally given the shape that is as close to the finished product as humanly possible. During these times of hard labour of my brain, (I believe that is my own hard work, for you can't separate a man from his brain), I create the impression among the observers that I am idling. In a way, I am like the duck. The duck keeps calm and unruffled on the surface, but paddles like the devil underneath!

The time I take, finally, to tap out the article, which has been processed in my mind, is not much. That is the only time when the world sees me at work. That explains why people, who know me, who often have a chance to see me sitting at the work table believe that hard work and I just are not made for each other.

That conclusion is baseless.

It is a conclusion arrived at on the basis of observed features which, at least in my case, do not speak much of the grinding that my brain undergoes during the creative process.

Creativity is perhaps, the hardest type of work in which one can indulge. I know, beyond doubt, that I work really hard. That is all that matters. For, I do not depend on confidential reports or annual work performance assessments to keep me going. I am my own master. And I do just the work that I enjoy doing.

You may call me anything—idler, shirker, *kaamchor*... and I shall not bat even an eyelid, for I know how hard I work. Hard work does not kill anybody. And that truth is very much ingrained in me. So, here I go, tapping out yet another skit.

Man in the rut

Am I a man who can be exhibited as the finest example of a human who is caught in a rut? If that be the case, I shall not even bat an eyelid, what to talk of batting both my eyelids.

Gavaskar, Tendulkar, Lara and other top batsmen, may feel the link between their batting and that of the eyelid, none too complimentary. They may even demand that the word, batting shall be exclusively reserved for the sportsmen, that some suitable word may be attached to the up and down motion of the eyelids. They may even justify the demand that since reservation is nothing new, since the entire people of this nation are demanding all sorts of reservations, those who have reservations about the policy of reservation, which gives merit back seat, too are pleading for reservation that goes with quality, competency and skill), there should be no difficulty in extending this special facility sought by the cricketers. However, at the moment, their plea is only getting off the ground. It will take a long time before the powers agree to this demand. Till then, I can bat my eyelid, without anyone telling me that I am violating any of the basics of the Indian Constitution. The honour enthralls me, makes me feel right on top of the world. Years ago, when I was a student, one of our teachers gave us a tip. He said, "Whatever you do, do it perfectly." The barber who does a perfect job and nips off just the bristles which have grown longer than they should or which stand out where they ought not, is doing a perfect job. And he, sooner than later, shall be dated by Presidents and Prime Ministers and shall even put up a poster which may read, 'By order to the President of India' or 'Prime Minister's hairdresser' or something equally effective.

And, then, it struck me that the man who seeks excellence sticks to his field. He goes over and over again performing nothing new. All that he does is go round and round, very much like the oxen which turn the oil mill, drawing deeper ruts on the ground, making the rut his own. In the process, if he is capable, he lends to the rut certain individual distinctions. He makes the rut gain immense attention. The onlookers begin to see creative spurts in the rut. With every passing day, more and more people gather around the scene where the dedicated operator pursues his profession and gives better indentations to the rut.

The audience cheer the man because they see, in the rut, much more than what the creator who wallows in the rut espies. The cue cannot be missed. Perfection is for those who know how to be in the rut. They are not jack of all trades. They do not fitter away their energies, chasing will-ó-the-wisps. They stick to their ruts, make them exclusive, distinctive, highly individualistic.

What is M F Husain doing, but, moving deeper into the intricacies of the rut of creativity? Did not Mahatma Gandhi find greatness by drawing the rut of social reformation and political emancipation? What is Medha Patekar doing but etching her imprints on the roll of honour by fighting for the protection of the people affected by the Narmada Dam?

So, when someone thinks I am a man in the rut, I feel elated. I look upon the comment as a tribute. I know that someone has started noticing the rut I have made; it is an indication that the future is bright. That is a thought that cheers.

◆◆◆

Perky Profiles

Ask any man who is the most dangerous specimen of humanity and he will unhesitatingly reply that the secretary of the ladies' club is the one who causes him the maximum trouble.

He holds her responsible for domestic disturbances and financial ruin. If he could muster courage, he would put her to the stake. But, in this age of civilisation, he can do nothing more than repress his anger and shower abuses on her in private. She comes from a rich family and, therefore, is considered to be the epitome of fashion. By becoming the secretary of the ladies' club, she forges ahead and steals the show. She becomes the leader whom other ladies follow meekly. The members of the club have only one aim, the subjugation of the male. It is their complaint that man holds authority and that woman has been denied her due share. So, they want to wage a battle to trim down the male and to assert the supremacy of the female. They ask why a woman should rot in the kitchen, handling vegetables, preparing dishes, washing napkins, ironing shirts, while a man enjoys the best of both worlds.

Being the wife of a high official, the secretary has a host of servants to attend to the children and the master of the house. She holds the view that men are born to provide facilities for their better half and that a husband who fails to release his wife from domestic chores, is not worth the title of a 'husband'. She educates other members and brings them round to her point of view. She advises them to fight for their rights.

She arranges a meeting daily at the residence of one of the members. Here, the members discuss the latest fashions, expose the defects and foibles of their husbands and try to devise methods to wean their husbands from their erring ways.

It is the secretary who provides magazines like *Cosmo*, *Femina*, *Women's era* and other publications of interest to the ladies. She is the first to adopt the fashions and designs elaborately set out in these journals. Nothing changes faster than her hairstyle. Today, it is coloured, parted in the middle and deftly plaited. After a week, she pulls the hair into a large-size beehive, thriving at the very top of her skull. A month later, she goes for some other hair colour and cut.

The hair parlours of the town are happy for they have a rolling trade as other women, immediately, follow the leadership of the secretary.

She gets designer outfits from abroad through the friends of her husband posted in foreign countries. She displays her acquisitions and sows desire in the minds of the members of the club. This leads to domestic discord at many homes. The wives demand similar outfits; the husbands either gather courage to deny the request and stick to the decision bravely; or they yield and become mendicants.

She has the habit of walking into your house when you are about to doze off. It is a holiday. Your plans are upset by the secretary. Your wife pushes you forward and introduces you to the secretary.

There is a strange gleam in her eyes when she surveys you. You don't smell trouble. You talk to her casually and withdraw, leaving the ladies to have a private talk. You go happily to your bed. It is then that you hear the secretary muttering, "That man of yours needs some exercise. He's too stout."

That does the trick. After the secretary leaves, your wife points out that you are fat, that she is putting you on a diet. All delicacies are taboo. You are fed on bread, biscuits and toasts so that you wonder whether life is worth living at all. You are ordered to rotate your torso at impossible angles and to run a couple of miles daily, early in the morning, on an empty stomach.

It is her little, apparently innocuous, statements which spell trouble. She takes upon herself the duty of attending to the welfare of the members and advises them how to teach manners to husbands, how to make them tend the baby when the baby cries, how to bend and bow to the will of their wives.

The only redeeming feature is that she tries these tricks on her husband before she disseminates the ideas. It is however impossible to escape her. She controls you through your wife.

She may rightly be called, 'The remote control.'

The better half

IT is difficult to decide her age. She may be a cute and young bundle of curves, with charming looks and velvety skin. Or, she may be fat and stout with a few streaks of grey hair which she tries without success to conceal. Or, she may be withered, with sagging chin and toothless smile, ambling along with wobbly steps. Whatever be her age, she is the better half. Immediately after marriage, she accepts this title with great confidence and attunes herself to the role. It becomes her firm conviction that the world's most under-developed territory lies concealed under the skull of her husband. No man, she argues, who is sane and sensible, will enter matrimony when the odds are so heavily weighted against him. No wonder, she is the better half. And it is her duty to protect her worse half.

Her first job after entering wedlock is to assert her authority. This is done surreptitiously when the man's intellect and commonsense have reached abysmal depths. His vision and ideals are clouded by the new-found love. "Wouldn't her darling love to be free from the botheration of managing the house? Wouldn't he prefer to leave the budgeting to her? Oh, she would, indeed, be happy to take up all these burdens on her shoulders, so that her husband may enjoy a carefree existence. Only, he must handover his pay packet to her." The worse half is lured by all these sweet words. He swallows the bait along with the hook. In a moment of weakness, he agrees to her proposal. She has won the major battle in claiming her supremacy.

After the funds pass into her hands, she acts like a dictator. She redrafts the budget in such a way that heavy economy is introduced in the spending of her husband. The saving thus effected is diverted cleverly towards the purchase of saris and cosmetics which satiate her caprices. When her husband accuses her of extravagance, she denies the charge vehemently and brings further strength to her argument with torrential tears which are defined as feminine water power that defeats masculine will power.

She still wears the mantle of docility and fans the ego of her husband by cooing that she is only his shadow, that he is dearer to her than her own life. Her aim in life, she says, is to serve her master and to make life easy and pleasant for him. Thus, by mixing threats and platitudes, she pecks her husband till the world at large knows that he is henpecked. Almost simultaneously, a bald patch appears on the back of his head, in the area where the hen has pecked, often with metallic plates and heavy rolling pins. This is the stage when she discards the mantle of docility and reveals her true colours.

It becomes a habit with her to telephone her husband in the office and remind him to get a kilogram of sugar. "Don't forget. Otherwise, you'll have to drink your coffee without sugar." Even God can't save the husband who fails to bring the required article.

Often, she forces him to accompany her on one of her shopping sprees. She spends his hard-earned money without any qualms. Then, she walks ahead waving her vanity bag, as her poor husband drags along his weary frame, burdened with all the items purchased by his better half. Invariably, she meets one of her long-lost friends with whom she stands in a corner and talks for an hour, blissfully ignorant that her husband is almost on the point of collapse under the weight. When, at last, she bids goodbye and returns to her husband, she mutters in a tone that one adopts to placate a howling dog: "My, my! I'm so sorry I took so much time. It's Malati. She was with me in college. I had not met her for the last ten years. You're not angry, darling, are you?" She knows he is fuming with anger, ready to explode like a volcano. But she wards off the ugly scene with her apologetic words.

If a tap leaks in the house, it is her husband who can and should fix it. The lawn is to be mowed, the fan needs cleaning and oiling, the sofa is to be polished—well, who else will do these odd jobs, but her man? In her eyes, he is the all-in-one servant whom she must keep eternally in motion so that he may not become lazy and indolent.

She expects her husband to remember her birthday, but not her age. When her children act wisely and earn the approval of others, she remarks proudly, "Well, after all, they're mine." But, when they fail to come up to her expectations, she mutters, "You are all chips of the old block ... absolutely useless."

Even a lie, when it is repeated often enough, wears the garb of truth. By incessant repetition, she makes her husband swallow the lie that he is an intellectual bankrupt. At last, the husband is converted to her viewpoint. This is the moment of triumph. For, she has really become the better half.

Dictator's delight

You could not have missed the sweet, young thing, wearing skintight apparel and plunging neck line, ambling along to the bus stop, her face coated with umpteen layers of powder, her lips shaded according to her whims, with a devil-may-care attitude when she negotiates the crossings. She could be held responsible for some of the traffic accidents in our major cities. She infests the cities and scrupulously avoids the country. Motorists strain their necks to catch a fleeting glance of this graceful maiden, whose dress reveals much more than it conceals. Scooterists, cyclists and pedestrians vie with each other to get an eyeful and in the process, collide against each other, creating confusion.

It is rumoured that the status of a steno is judged by the number of accidents she causes.

She always carries a vanity bag, inside which is packed an assortment of articles needed to keep her exterior from wearing off and bringing out into focus the undesirable and the ugly interior. Deprive her of the handbag and she behaves like a fish out of water.

She has perfected the art of boarding the bus. She does not rush madly at the entrance to the bus. From a distance, she looks coyly at the conductor. The conductor is enraptured by the look and goes out of the way to accommodate her.

Once inside the bus, she prefers to stand rather than sit, even on vehicles which have seats reserved for ladies.

Not that she has any doubts about her femininity. There is more pleasure in sitting by the side of a smart, well-built young man who is ready to enjoy every moment of life. As soon as she gets this chance, she takes the seat, pulls out a Perry Mason novel and poses as if she is reading the novel. She encourages some fun from her neighbour provided he plays within limits.

She is not a ravishing beauty. But, among an army of men in office, she is the only colourful personality. She causes male hearts to flutter. Those who are married feel they have made fools of themselves by entering matrimony before seeing this bundle of modernity. The unmarried are hopeful that she may choose one of them as her partner and spare no effort to wriggle into her good books.

But, she encourages no approaches till she is certain of the income and status of the individual.

She has the inside information of all that is happening in the office. What she does not know is not worth knowing. She acts like a one-man-information centre, letting out news in bits, making it impossible for anyone individual to make head or tail of them.

She can pull fast ones on her colleagues. She specially revels on All Fools' Day. She is firmly of the view that all men are fools, that they are endowed with brains of very poor quality. In support of her opinion, she recites instances when some charming stenos had bagged their bosses as husbands and could dictate terms to their former bosses. This, she says, is the most effective way to turn the tables. From being the delightful recipients of dictation, these stenos have become delights of the dictators.

Her actions are not always above board. She is only waiting for a chance to hook a mate. If it could be the boss himself, it is most desirable. There are dangers, of course, like the unexpected entry of the boss's wife when she is perched on the boss's lap. But, the consummate skill of the steno is ready to meet any situation. She explains that the compromising situation should not be misunderstood by the lady, that she was only trying to relieve the muscular pain of the boss by loading her weight on the point of pain.

There was a time when ladies used to rule the house, rocking babies, attending to household duties, playing second fiddle to their husbands.

But, the lady steno who has ousted man from the profession started by Ganeshji, the Lord with the pot belly, who came to the rescue of Vyasa in transcribing the Mahabharata, now rocks the offices and in the act, becomes the **dictator's dictator**.

She is always aware of her goal. And, she knows how to reach it. She does not rest till she hooks her man.

Bull in a China shop

She has no business to enter the Brabourne Stadium, yet walks in on the pretext of watching the test match. She is blissfully ignorant of the rules of cricket. The terminology used by cricketers is Greek and Latin to her. To add to all these is the fact that she is not physically fit to sit under the blazing sun, watching a game that gives her little or no entertainment.

Her husband is not keen to take her along with him. But she brings in all the tricks of femininity and makes him take her along.

The crowd gives her the first shock. She loses her poise when she fails to spot any of her friends with whom she could have spent the whole day, gossiping. She takes her seat and surveys the scene with apparent disgust.

The play begins. The husband is engrossed in the game when she mutters, "Darling. Do you like this pattern that I have knitted?"

"Oh. Very nice."

"You've not even bothered to glance at it."

"Don't disturb me. We have come to witness the Test match, not to appreciate your knitting patterns."

"Why do you lose your temper? After all cricket is not that important. It's only a stupid game about which Bernard Shaw has . . . . ."

"I'm not interested in Shaw's opinion. Leave me in peace to enjoy the game."

"Cricket's a dull game."

"I didn't force you to come."

"How can I enjoy the game unless you tell me the intricacies of the game. Tell me, darling, what're those two men in white overcoats doing there? They seem to do nothing else except stretch their hands occasionally, so that the bowler may hang his coat or sweater. Why does one or other of them bend, stoop low and look at the stumps as if the heavens are about to fall?"

"They are the umpires. Now, sit tight. I'm missing the game because of your chatter."

"Can't I ask some simple questions? You don't love me."

"Don't start an argument. I love you."

"Then tell me, does a leg spinner spin his legs when he bowls?"

"What gave you the idea?"

"I guessed so."

"Wrong."

"Everything is wrong in cricket. Take, for instance, the wicket keeper."

"What's wrong about him?"

"It's the batsman who protects the wicket, preventing the vicious fast balls and the cunning spinning balls from dislodging the bails and the wickets. He should be called the wicket keeper. On the other hand, the wicket keeper indulges in acts of wanton destruction. On many occasions, he has deliberately kept the ball in his hand and uprooted the stumps. He has watched with a broad smile when a fielder threw the ball at the stumps."

"Will you stop this rot or not?"

"Now let us take batting. A great batsman, you say, should make all his strokes, keeping the ball on the ground. Yet, when he makes the ball scorch the earth and cross the boundary, he gets only four runs. The moment he throws the principle of keeping the ball on the ground overboard, making the ball float in the air and land beyond the boundary line, he gets six runs."

"Shut up!"

"I'm only pointing out the flaws in the game."

"You can do it later."

"I'm getting bored. Let us go home."

"Let stumps be drawn for the day. Then we'll go."

"Then, you'll have to listen to my views on cricket till evening."

"Well. I yield. Let us go."

The man follows his wife, mumbling blasphemies; his face reminds one of the broken Chinaware after the bull had a merry go. And, the wife presents the very picture of an arrogant bull. She is a grade above the bull in the China shop. For, she plays with animate objects while the proverbial bull is satisfied with the Chinaware.

Travel Travail

The last laugh

My wife and I board the trailer to take a round of Magnolia Plantation, 20 kms off Charleston, South Carolina, US. "The trailer will wind its way through the exotic swamps and lakes, overlooked by towering oaks and redwoods of Magnolia plantation," says the tour conductor, while checking our tickets. Then he adds, "I am a multi-purpose man. I am the driver, conductor and the tourist guide too."

The trailer cuts through a path bordered by shrubs and trees. The conductor details the history of the family that owns the plantation and lists the infinite variety of flowering plants in the area. The trailer rolls on. So do his words. They take swift turns and sharp swings, slide over jokes or witty comments that evoke laughter from the tourists on board. "We're now approaching the swamps. Get ready to see a variety of birds, some turtles and a few alligators", he announces. Then he adds, "Keep your hands and legs well within the trailer. This is the kingdom of the alligators. They have one weakness. They snap at anything that dangles and is within reach." Hurriedly, arms and legs are drawn in.

The wheels groan when the trailer takes a sharp turn, skirting the lake. "Soon the alligators will be sighted. The alligator can notch speeds up to 30 miles per hour on a straight course; but it can't turn around quickly. So better zigzag if you want to leave the alligator far behind," he pauses, providing time for his message to sink in. Then he jokes, "Some experts say that if you play dead or peer into the alligator's eyes, sternly, the alligator will back away. I don't know. I have never tried."

We keep a look out for alligators, but none turns up. The conductor repeats his message. "They never fail to appear. They will come, for sure."

The trailer moves on. Still no alligator. One young man, behind our seats, quips, "This is a memorable ride. The conductor is taking us for a ride, when he says there are alligators around in these waters."

The conductor replies, "It is your time to laugh. But, I will have the last laugh, for sure. The alligators never fail me."

We are more than half way on the road skirting the lake. Suddenly, we hear the happy notes of the conductor, "Look, there they are, two fine young alligators."

Our eyes zero in on the amphibians. One of them quickly slips in, splashes the water and vanishes. The second one lazily lies on the sand, inert and immobile.

The conductor laughs aloud happily waving to the alligator, saying, "See you later, alligator."

Therooflesslady

The aircraft bounces a couple of times at touch down and races along the tarmac, while we, the passengers, hail the feat with wild applause, creating the impression that it is the first time that a pilot has ever managed to bring an airborne object down to terra firma. Perhaps, there is much to the applause than what we read into it. A reality check tells me that the applause is an expression of our gratitude to the pilot, who is the God, who holds our lives in his hand, while we take to flight, for bringing us safe and sound back to this earth where we rightfully belong. The plane rolls on, circles, loses speed, finally edges its way, adjusting its belly parallel to the gateway and comes to a dead stop, and waits for the huge door of the aircraft to get fully aligned with the duct. Suddenly, the inside of the plane turns into a bustle of activities. Passengers work their way out to the narrow pathway, bump into each other while frantically pulling out their hand-luggage. They vie with each other to be the first to disembark. I decide that I shall spend the last few minutes, easing in the seat. "What's holding you back?" asks Miss Betty, the young vibrant girl of sixteen who has the aisle seat and has been sitting next to me during the long flight. Nine hours back, when we boarded the plane at Heathrow, Betty and l were strangers to each other. Now we are friends, who have spent nearly eight hours together. That gives her the right to fire that question at me.

"Is it you?" I tease her, knowing that she won't take it amiss because she is in the Spring of her youth and I am in the Autumn of my old age, and hence, the two can coexist without creating complications. "I suspect it's your old legs, frozen into lead, due to long inactivity during the flight, that holds you back. Or are you reluctant to come face to face with the most famous lady of New York, who has no roof over her head," Betty gets up, stretches her hand to fetch her small suitcase, tucked in the overhead hold, now that the crowd has virtually melted. She also pulls out my briefcase, moves aside to give me space to wriggle out from between the seats to the narrow path that shall take us to the exit, "Thank you," I pick up my briefcase. While we make it to the exit, I ask her, "Tell me. Betty you talked about the famous lady without a roof over her head. Are you, by any chance, speaking of Hillary Clinton, who is now the Senator from New York? Is she yet to get a house here?" Betty's laughter ripples like the cascades of a mountain stream. I wait for her to free herself from the grips of whatever it be that has tickled her. Finally, she finds her words. "There you go wrong. Mrs Clinton has a spacious house at New York. The most famous lady who has no roof over her head is..." Betty takes a meaningful pause, while she walks along the duct, with me close on her trail, before she breaks the spell with the words, "The Statue of Liberty."

Travel trouble

When I confide in Suren, my friend, a travel-tanned veteran, if ever there is one, my plans for a holiday in Europe, with my better half on tow, he says, "Good luck". Have fun time... "Thank you," I smile before I notice that he has not yet completed whatever it is that he wants to say and mutter a note of regret. "Forget it," he ducks, perhaps realising, on second thoughts, that what he wants to convey is best left unsaid. But I don't let him get away with that. He has roused my curiosity. Once curiosity determines to work its way through, I believe it is not the feline alone that gets a deadly jolt, but even humans. Unwilling to face the risk, I beg Suren to share with me whatever it is that, because of premature intrusion, is cut short. "I hope your travel plans have been well coordinated," he asks. "I have friends at London, Paris, Berlin and Amsterdam. They will play host, happily. For they know as much as I know that fish and guest get stale after three days. I have made it known to them that I shall not spend more than three days with them because 1 have the whole of Europe to cover in a fortnight. I propose to hire a car for a fortnight and drive through. I have already collected the road maps and propose to train my wife to operate as the navigator. We shall, of course, visit the tower of London, watch the change of guards at Buckingham Palace, take a boat ride on the Thames, stand atop Eiffel and get a bird's eye view of Paris, visit Louvre, go through the tunnel where Princess Diana breathed her last...," I remember that I am carrying coal to Newcastle and shift the topic,

"I have gained enough vocabulary of French, German and Spanish to see me through," I arrest my words. "Sounds great!" Suren is brief. "But you don't sound quite enthusiastic," I note his reticence and decide to get to the root of the matter. "Well, you will enjoy your tour if you display the spirit of adventure, be ready to handle unexpected hitches with confidence. For even the best of plans may go awry. Take, for example, this experience of a Swiss gentleman, looking for directions, pulls up at a bus stop and inquires of two men waiting for the bus, *"Entschuldigung, koennen Sie Deutsch sprechen?"* All that he gets are blank stares. *"Excusez-moi, pariez vous Francais?"* he tries. Once again he gets blank stares. *"Parlare Italiano?"* No response. *"Hablan ustedes Espanol?"* Still nothing. The Swiss guy drives off, extremely disgusted, unaware that the men were American tourists. The first American then turned to the second and said: "Maybe, we should learn a foreign language." "Why?" asked the other. "That guy knew four languages, and it didn't do him any good." Get it? Suren laughs, once he notices that his comment has tickled me and I am ready to enjoy the joke.

Camera-shy

THERE is a certain amount of mistiness in the air as I step out of the Hiltons in Paris, eager to stomp around the Eiffel Tower.

I had checked in at the hotel around noon on November 30.

After a quick lunch, I pick up my camera and make a beeline for the towering monument which is a product of love built by a pioneering engineer named Ferdinand de Lesseps, who was then considered mad to have gone in for such a complex steel structure, fabricated out of bars, nuts and bolts.

It takes me less than five minutes to reach the foot of the Eiffel Tower. I crane my neck, letting my eyes slowly move up the contours of the tower.

From every angle, it looks perfectly shaped. There is no oddity, no strangeness, no unbecoming bulge or dip anywhere in the structure. For more than a hundred years, informs the guide, who's an old Indian staying at Paris now for over two decades and speaks French with perfect diction. He is from Pondicherry, once a French colony.

He says that the tower had been the most individualistic monument around. He adds, "There had been common who made their pot of gold by 'selling off' the Tower. There had been bold and daring characters who had used the tower as the base for their stunt shows."

I gape, craning my neck, eager to see the tower taper off. I find several people, working their way to the top of the tower; some of them, who had scaled greater heights, look to me like ants edging their way through.

The arch, which has a grace, provides the basic support. The arches on all four sides are of equal dimensions, says my guide. I nod, while making a futile bid to see the tip of the tower.

That is when I realise that there is a vagueness about the top. I notice a sort of cloudy, patchy mist which crowns the tower. The middle limbs of the tower, too, are cloaked in a sort of misty milky white. It is only the lower tiers of the tower which are perceptible.

That makes me wince.

I had hopes of snapping the Eiffel Tower on film. I had been excited at the prospect. But one look at the tower is enough to convince me of the futility of trying to record the monument on film... on this day anyway, anyhow.

My guide reads my thought.

He steps in and says that I can have a few snaps of the tower from unusual angles, so long as I do not dare to film anything other than the lower tiers. The mist, he tells me, has not descended too low. Soon, however, the mist shall envelop the entire structure. Then there would be nothing for me to film.

I nod my head.

We move further away from the tower.

I hand over the camera to my friend. He makes me pose under a tree which has shed all its leaves, leaving its branches dry and listless, as though stretching their hands out for a gift of fresh life (which shall not come till winter peters off), while adjusting the camera. Finally, he clicks!

Now he makes me shift to a new location, assume a new posture while taking yet another snapshot.

After taking about six shots, my guide tells me that I should now be happy!

I wink and assert, "I never thought the tower shall be camera-shy. But, today, it appears to be. So, I could only record its lower limbs. The tower has its head in the clouds. And the clouds have thrown a veil over the tower."

I manage to board the bus, which, as usual, does not stop at the bus stop, but a few yards... Sorry! A few metres... off the scheduled place.

The bus starts moving, even as I manage a toe-hold on the footboard of the bus, half my body hanging out, trying to work out the redefined location of my body's centre of gravity, holding out, beyond doubt, the possibility of a fall, which shall prove as disastrous to me as the one which befell Jack and Jill who went up the hill to fetch a pail of water and tumbled.

Jack, says the nursery rhyme, fell down and broke his crown. (Better a broken crown than a broken skull, says someone. I am not quite so certain. I have a nagging suspicion that the crown here refers to the poor boy's skull). Jill came tumbling after. We don't know what happened to Jill, but it is my belief that she sustained severe bruises and also cracked her forehead.

I hang on, with all the strength my hands can command. With superhuman efforts, I avert a fall. Then, I heave myself in and squeeze my way to the august presence of the conductor, who, however, crowded the bus be, has a safe place to rest his seat.

With great difficulty, I get close to the conductor. I glower at him, ask why he doesn't bother to check whether all the passengers, eager to get in, are safely on board before the bus moves. That makes him scared. He shoots out of his seat. He squirms and shows assumed politeness which makes me feel ill at ease. I am not accustomed to such humility from the man who lords it high in his bus. I wonder what has come over him. Am I seeing illusions? I rub my eyes to assure myself that it is not a dream.

The conductor, meanwhile, stands politely and enquires, "Ah, sir, pray, tell me who you are?"

"A common citizen, my man," I reply rather angrily.

"Everyone is a common commoner. Are you, by any chance, the Chairman of the DTC? I must know, sir, before I can serve you. For, I note that powers-that-be have taken a leaf from *Rajas* and *Maharajas* of yore. They now travel incognito. So,..." the conductor waits for my reply.

"Suppose I am the Deputy Chairman of the DTC," I stress the word, *"suppose"*—hoping that the conductor would not miss the cue.

But, the chap shivers from head to toe. He says, "Sorry, sir. If I had known, I would have, personally been at the footboard to give you a grand reception. I think I shall do that, in future. Stand at the footboard, have a garland, ready, to welcome the VIP... Now, dear sir, here is the ticket... "the conductor hands the ticket to me, duly marking it after finding out my destination, but refuses to take the charge.

"But, why?" I ask.

"Because you are what you said you are—the Chairman's right-hand man. Remember me, sir. I am Kharati Ram. I served you well today," he says.

"Do you serve others as well?" I ask.

"Now, sir. Is that possible, sir? In a democracy too, there are some people who are more equal than others. For some people, the bus will wait. Others wait for the bus.

To the first group, I show respect. From the other group, I command respect," he says.

"But, my friend, I am only a commoner. I only said suppose I am the Deputy Chairman of the DTC," I repeat.

"So, you are not travelling, incognito. My God! Get lost. Out of my sight, this very second," he screams and goes back to his seat, puts his left leg over the right and peers at me as if I do not exist.

Malayan wisdom

I am distressed when I learn that my friend, Anurag, has been overlooked by the Promotion Committee. I know he is a competent executive. He does his work quietly, strives for perfection, manages to clear all tasks assigned to him with competence. These are the qualities which ought to have helped him rise in the hierarchy.

Yet, I find that the man has been left out. It pains me.

I walk up to his cabin. He looks distraught. I can spot the pall of gloom which masks his face. He squeezes out a rather wan smile, when I greet him. He shakes my hand without much enthusiasm. It is clear that he is bleeding within.

It does not make sense to him.

He has been performing his duties with competency and efficiency. Yet, he has been dumped, while others, who were known to be easygoing and casual to their work, had been preferred.

"It is time you swing with the times," I tell him.

"You mean I must also become casual and indifferent to my work, let piles of paper form a heap on my table?" Anurag asks wryly.

"Oh, no. But, the trouble with you is that you work, quietly. You do it in silence. You don't go about, telling the seniors, whenever the chance comes, how you have tackled a difficult problem, how you have worked out a solution to an impasse, how you surmounted a catch 22 situation," I tell him.

"Why should I tell them? They are there to identify my merit. The files I have handled go to my seniors. So...." Anurag wonders where he has gone wrong.

"That's not enough, my dear," I comment.

"But, why"?

"Because, these days, nobody has time to identify the merits of others. In a way, we are living in an age of publicity. One has not only to be good, but also tell the whole world that one is good. Every successful man, every successful industrial group or business concern revels in telling the whole world about his/its achievements. Self advertisement is the trick through which successful people scale greater heights, which big industrial groups adopt to improve their sales and to increase their profits," I clarify.

"You mean I must go about, telling all and sundry about my work attitude, my triumphs, my successes?" Anurag is not convinced.

"Exactly. You can't avoid it. If you don't tell about yourself, who will do it for you? I won't do it, when I too am your competitor and the slots available at the higher level are fewer. You have to do it. And you must do it because basically, you are good at your work, and nobody can have any reason to think you are indulging in a self-ad campaign because of your proven worth," I tell him.

"I have never done it, all these years. Not at college, where I used to be counted among the best students. Not here, during the last three years of work. And, now, you want me to change?" Anurag is still sceptical.

"You must. And, if you want to rise to your level of

incompetency, as Peter shall put it, you must mix hard work with self-advertisement too." I insist.

"My God!" Anurag sighs.

"To help you, I can offer a working model. Take the cue from the hen. What does the hen do? Brings the house down, informs the whole world that it has laid an egg. The turtle, on the other hand, lays a thousand eggs, but chooses to keep a stiff upper lip. So we know about the hen and its productive activities. Be like the hen, not like the turtle. Or, so says the Malayan proverb," I spot a slight smile that indicates that Anurag has got the message.

A Victorian tale

SUBODH and I walk round the Victoria Memorial, at a very leisurely pace. I am viewing the monument for the first time and hence, am taken in by the distinct features of the memorial, as much as the commentary by Subodh, my friend and host.

"The memorial is the pride of Calcutta," Subodh says, when we finally turn away.

"The pride may be yours, but prouder still must be Queen Victoria. For the memorial carries her name," I point out.

"What's in a name?" Subodh pouts his lips.

"Queen Victoria did not think so. She lent her name liberally. This memorial carries her name and she has every right to feel honoured. As a Calcuttan, you have every right to feel proud too. The Queen gave her name readily to many other things. Remember the Victoria, the horse-drawn carriage, which was once the centre of attraction in the heart of Bombay, the Flora Fountain area?"

"Even that Victoria had its humble origin here, in Calcutta," Subodh's words floor me. "Are there no limits to your loyalty to Calcutta?" I tease.

"This is not false loyalty, my friend. The bughee owes its all to the strike by palanquin bearers in 1828. The strike inconvenienced many people, especially the officials of the East India Company," Subodh peers at me, explaining, "Among the Britishers was one Mr Brownlow.

He did not like to walk to office. And he never felt safe riding a horse."

"Not everyone is safe on them. Often a horse dislodges its mount. Perhaps, Brownlow was not white enough. And even among browns, he came low. The horse would have brought him lower still," I play with the name Brownlow.

"You and your weird sense of humour," Subodh snaps at me, stifling a smile. Then he adds, "Brownlow examined the palanquin. He viewed it from all angles, then engaged a carpenter to add a pair of shafts and four wheels to it. The carpenter completed the job in a few days and Brownlow drove the strange contraption, drawn by a pony, to his office, in style. Others took the cue. The new vehicle, which was named Brownberry, replaced the palanquin," says Subodh.

"What has that got to do with the Victoria of Bombay?" I ask.

"The Victoria of Bombay was an improved design of the Brownberry," Subodh asserts.

I accept his words since I find Subodh's logic tenable. Further, I am a good guest. A good guest never offends his host who, in this case, is Subodh.

Tongue-twister

The passenger train crawls to a stop at Karisuzhndamangalam. A few people try to get off, but are blocked by a handful of passengers eager to board the train. I watch, amused at the stalemate that the push and the pull create at the door. "Hi, take a look at the name of the station," My friend Col Vinod Chopra nudges me. This is his first trip to the south. He has chosen me to be his aide-de-camp, escort, guide, mentor, all rolled into one, during the leisurely train journey by a passenger train that heads further south of Madurai, the temple town whose presiding deity is Goddess Meenakshi. He makes a valiant effort to read the name of the station, but fumbles. But he doesn't give up easily. He tries again and again. His frantic attempt to get the name right reminds me of Robert Bruce, the king who lost his crown and didn't know how to regain it till the spider showed him the way. Bruce learnt that success goes with tenacity. "Try, try till you succeed," he muttered to himself. This never-say-die attitude is what I spot in Vinod's attempts to spell the name right.

I watch him taking the name Karisuzhndamangalam, while the train shakes off its lethargy, lets out a long hoot and starts crawling. That works wonders. Those who want to get out scramble madly and land on the platform flinging their arms, holding bags or briefcases or sacks, staggering like drunks before finding their balance. Those who want to get in reach out for the handle, just manage to get footholds, before they squeeze their way in at great odds. The sight tickles me. I laugh out loud.

"Hi, are you laughing at me, just because I can't get the name right? Vinod growls and drives my funny thoughts out instantly. "Can't get what right?" I ask. "The name of this remote place. That combination 'ZH' is impossible to get right," his eyes reflect his discomfiture. "Impossible is a word that Napoleon struck off from his dictionary," I joke. "That belief felled him at Waterloo," Vinod battles me with that sharp bite. "Who wants a loo where water isn't available," I play with the name. "No joke, this. Tell me how to pronounce that combination 'ZH'?" he insists. I tell him how to hold his lips and his tongue to produce the sound. He stumbles, falters, but tries again and again till he gets a passable version of 'ZH'. "This town has a tongue twister for a name," Vinod shapes up the corners of his moustache and sharpens them before trying once again to get the pronunciation of the deadly combination, 'ZH' right.

Casually, turning the pages of the dictio nary, I get fascinated by the word, 'over'. It stands out as one of the words, which has found maximum liaisons.

The touch of casanova, in the word, 'over', is what strikes me most, I run down the pages, find that there is hardly any word in the language which has not linked itself with the word, 'over'. In the process, these words have gained new meanings, strong undertones, wide-ranging imports, throbbing vitality.

I can affirm that I am not overrating the word. Nor am I overreaching the limits of sensibility. I am convinced that the word, 'over', by nature, is overbearing. Those who get to know its power are overawed. It can be overcome, only when we get over the fear and cease to get overexcited over 'over'. Then comes the abiding faith in the friendly attitude of the word that draws .... does it overdraw into its fold, find delight in having a harem of words, in raising a herd of new words which expand the vocabulary of the language .... unto itself every word that is worth courting. I am not overestimating this date-ability of the word. The time has come to pay the word, a tribute that is its due. Nay! the tribute is overdue. Over and over again, do I run into words which owe their all to 'over'. I find 'over' overlaying itself, again and again. I find words like 'overlook' and 'overtake' and 'overdo' and 'overact' and 'overpower', parading themselves before me, hinting that I may spend ages without ever coming to know all the words which carry the genetic strain of the word, 'over'. They wink and laugh and dance while making me admit that the word, 'over' has sent its tentacles deep into the very marrow of the language, has left, in its trail, new words, laden with its stamp, ever reminding mankind that one can never get over the feeling that 'over' is the word that matters.

In its simplest form, the word indicates a sort of authority. Anybody who is over is occupying an elevated status. It represents hierarchial ranking. A senior has the power over his junior. In another incarnation, it denotes something that is done with. It implies 'finis'. 'The show is over' is a phrase that has subtle undertones may denote what it stands for, i.e. the end of a film or a play or a concert. It may indicate the death of a colourful personality. It may be brought in to indicate that the trick has been seen through.

Will the war in the Gulf region ever be over? The Foreign Minister of Israel seems to be a Cassandra in his approach. He has reviewed the situation, taken an overview of the present parleys, let his thoughts overflow. Here is what he says, "It's not over till it's over. Its not even over when it's over." I think here he has overshot the mark. Or perhaps, he has overexposed what he has in mind. By over sight, he has dropped the guard and overstepped the limits set for politicians. When he says that 'it's not even over when it's over', he is in projecting a threatening posture. Does he mean that Israel shall not let the peace parleys overweigh all else? Will he overthrow the terms of peace, so that his prediction that all is not over, as far as hostilities in the Gulf region are concerned, can come true?

Over to you to explore and find out the answer yourself. I have bowled the word 'over' to you. I hope it ends up as a maiden over, which brings me a wicket too.

◆◆◆

Random
Reflections

In praise of the kerchief

Taking things for granted comes naturally to man. (How can I, a *homo sapien*, let this secret out? says a friend. His nose twitches, his face contorts with anger, his lips flutter explosively. He gives me the impression that he is about to whip up a massive public protest against my comment. It hurts him, because it is a truth which man tries to cover up. It is one truth which every man knows, yet rarely ever admits. However, truth has to be out. And if I am the chosen instrument through whom this nugget of truth shall see the light of the day, so be it).

This realisation that man takes things for granted comes to me when I dab my face, streaming with sweat, with the kerchief. The strip of cloth, hardly 30 cms by 30 cms, mops up the sweat readily. It doesn't raise even the mildest of protest when I expect it to give my face a facelift. The kerchief does it with effortless ease. It gets sodden. It becomes a little less prim and trim. But the kerchief doesn't raise even the slightest objection. On the contrary, I find it performing the task with quiet confidence. It does a good job, when I press it firmly on spots where the grime and the dirt are maximum. My face becomes clean, presentable while the kerchief suddenly becomes dirty and shabby.

The kerchief thus becomes the carrier of other people's dirt. We hail Jesus for readily carrying the sins of others on his shoulders. By the same standard, the kerchief must be judged. It maintains a happy mien even when it carries the dirty look because of the transfer, we men manage to bring about, a transfer by which we look clean and the kerchief becomes laden with dirt.

If this is the only service which the kerchief renders to man, one may snipe, "Well, if the kerchief can't perform the one task assigned to it, we won't date it. And a whole arena of industry that thrives on producing this utility item shall be forced to down the shutters. So let not the kerchief get ideas of being one with the great redeemer who carries the sins of the world on his shoulders."

But, I can point out a variety of other services, the kerchief renders. I go to a function in a Gurudwara. I need something to cover up my head. Suddenly, I remember the kerchief. Out it comes, ready to go over my head.

I join a group of mourners. Many near relatives are sobbing. Tears well up in their eyes. Lo! It is the kerchief which each one turns to wipe off the tears. I find one man, holding the kerchief close to his eyes, even though his eyes sparkle. There is not even a drop of tear anywhere around, yet, by holding the kerchief close to his eyes, he creates an impression that he is cracking under the strain of grief.

How effective the kerchief is when you spot a creditor, as you walk along the shopping avenue, needs no elaboration. Everyone knows how the kerchief, held deftly over the eyes, creating the impression that you are giving the face, the lift it needs, conceals one's identity and gives not even the slimmest of chances to the creditor to spot you and to waylay you and insist on his pound of flesh.

Hold a scented kerchief, over the nose, and you can negotiate the terrain which is laden with the foulest of stench. Reach for the kerchief when smoke makes you cough and choke. I can go on, forever, singing the praise of the kerchief.

◆◆◆

Palm-top legacy

The TV shows a farmer in Vietnam, tilling the land in torrential rain, protecting himself with a golden coloured umbrella, woven with bamboo reeds. The parasol resembles the umbrella, made of palm leaf, used in the heartland of Travancore state (now part of Kerala) in the 1940s. Now hardly ever does one see this umbrella: wide-rimmed, with a gentle curvature on top, firmly ribbed by the spokes of the palm leaf, a neat slot on its underside to fit one's top and stay there.

Those were the days when the common umbrella, made of taffeta, was struggling for acceptance. It was compact but costly; well beyond the common man's means. Even those who could afford it found it hard to break away from the traditional umbrella, made by native artisans.

In those days, most families lived in homes set in an acre or two of land. Our family too lived in a large plot. The toilets stood at the rear of the house, separated from the living quarters by a hundred feet or more, linked by a narrow footpath running through thick vegetation. During the unusually severe monsoon in most parts of Travancore, when the need to visit the toilet became pressing, the new-fangled device proved a little less quick to respond; and at times, unreliable too. Its steel ribs often got in each other's way. When one tried to force the umbrella open, the ribs would revolt, break loose from the main stem or from one of the myriad joints. Eventually, one would hear a rip as one or more of the ribs punched large holes in the taffeta, making the umbrella useless against the rains.

The palm-leaf umbrella was not so wayward. Every house, even those with a pair of new, folding umbrellas, held a few palm leaf ones. They stayed neatly piled up at the back of the house, usually in a shed with a roof of thatched coconut leaves. One would hurry to the corner, pick up one of them and quickly slip it on one's head. It would sit there, firmly, while the wearer would step out into the open, daring the rain to do its worst. The umbrella would take the downpour; let the raindrops sing and dance on its top, and drip down to the wet ground, while protecting the wearer. Not a drop would fall on the person whom the umbrella had taken under its protection. It took its duty seriously, never played truant.

Today the palm-leaf umbrella has gone the way of the dodo.

A haunting mystery

I am not a scientist who gets baffled by every inexplicable phenomena that defies logic. Nor do I have anything in common with the housewife who ends up with an unexpected and hitherto untried new dish that the mix of *mirch* and *masala* and vegetables/meat or fish, held in a pot whose bottom is on fire, produces, tastes it, finds it immensely palatable and gets set to track down each step of the process with the tenacity of a Newton or an Einstein, so that she could replicate the effect and then patent the product. Given the chance, I shy away from mysteries. Thank God! They, except for a solitary exception, keep away from me. This solitary mystery has made life miserable for me. It haunts me, day in and day out. I try to turn my back to it, but it spins round me faster and winks at me, giving me the impression that it is challenging me to put it behind, indicating that it is more tenacious than even the old man who managed to get a perch on poor Sinbad's shoulders and refused to be dislodged. I whirl around, like a top, but the puzzle keeps pace with my rolls. Rolling around leaves me dizzy, but makes no impact on the mystery. I slow down like a top that loses its speed of rotations and starts wobbling and the mystery sneers at me.

"See, try to shake me off. And all that your efforts earn you are dizziness in your head and stumbles on your feet." Is this mystery then God itself? For God, they say, is here, there, and everywhere. He is *sarvavyapee*, says Prahlad. If that be the case, I can do no more than throw up my hands, ruing my mistake in taking on an all-powerful, all-filling enigma that is well beyond my powers to solve and pin down. Ah! I still have not defined this mystery. I should have done that, earlier. Right at the beginning. I didn't do that. Not my fault. My head is still reeling a bit. But it isn't reeling so fast that I can't think on my legs. I have regained the power to be logical. So here is the mystery that has stumped me. The mystery belongs to the world of telephones. When I try to get through to someone on phone, urgently, more often than not, I get connected to a wrong number. How come the wrong number is never engaged? Who will solve this mystery? May be, I should dump this puzzle in the lap of APJ Kalam. He is the man for the job. For he is our President. The President is duty bound to solve the problems the common man faces.

Let judges court rhyme

Practitioners of law may draw quotable quotes from law books and bound volumes of recorded judgements, delivered by erudite judges of courts from all around the globe, but they know that the legal system, truly draws strength and sustenance from common sense, which is buttressed by rhyme and reason. So my heart jumps with joy when I read about Judge J. Michael E Akin of Pennsylvania. Frequently, says the press report, he delivers his rulings in rhyme.

Here is one instance when he chose rhyme to dispose of a case. The accused didn't contest the charges. He said he rued his mistake. The judge noted that on the stand was a first-time offender. He, therefore, decided to be humane. He didn't send the accused to prison. Instead, he let the accused go, after warning him, "And so, I say, without fail,/Do this again and it's off to jail."

I wonder how much more enjoyable the scene at courts shall be if we have judges who use verses that have reason and rhyme while handing out judgements. That gives me a weird idea.

Suppose the law colleges revise the syllabi and add a section on poetic justice! That will open up more scope for employment for a horde of unemployed young poets, who have not yet made it to the top league. They may help the future judges get a feel of emotions.

Then it strikes me that poetry is emotion resurrected in tranquillity.

I know this is a mutilated version of an old quote. So nobody needs to tick me off for that aberration. A variation, deliberately introduced, is no aberration. It is just a parody. What's a parody but deft play with the original! It is not mutilation. Let those who think otherwise revise their stand. Let them not tell me, "Retract your stand. Or be ready to be taken to the court of law to answer the charge of assaulting the definition of poetry, replacing the word recollected with resurrected."

Their threat shall not put me off. I know I am on firm ground. I am ready to face the charge, if only they arraign me before a judge who knows reason and rhyme.

I can imagine how such a judge shall react. After listening to both sides, he shall versify his verdict thus. "Words, alas, do not, in dictionaries, live,/Nor do they even a casual nod give,/To the scholars, who, to make a living,/Impose rules of their own making,/What is a quote but the decocted wisdom/Of a writer, ruling high over his kingdom,/Not encircled by a moat or a wall/And hence, accessible to one and all,/ Where rights are not defended by the sword./For, the pen is mightier than the sword,/The writer knows a quote a pen creates,/When another pen recreates,/Gives parody a fresh lease of life./ So, why make this the issue for a strife?". Then, he shall send me off with the parting verse, "The world is always ready/To enjoy a truly great parody/That deftly turns words around/And evokes laughter all around."

I wonder why the Labour government of Britain has taken up the cudgels against musical chairs, the amusing and exciting game that rouses such excitement and gives such cheer at school functions! They have argued that the game encourages aggression, "because it is always the biggest and the strongest children who win." That is perhaps the joke of the century. In fact, it is the one game that gives a fair chance to the nimble and the alert. The fat and the stout are usually sidelined because they get the message that the music has ended a microsecond later than the one who has his ears tuned to catch the signal ahead of others. This game virtually discourages aggression, sharpens one's survival kit, gives a fair chance to the slim and the agile, holds the scale even between the brain and the brawn. Yet, the British government have geared themselves, gone for the jugular of the game that has music in its soul and makes children run round and round chairs set in circles keeping steps to the music. All because of a mistaken belief that the game encourages aggression. Why, oh why, can't they go against the one game that has aggression built into it, one whose body and soul form a pack of aggression. There is no room for anything else in this game that we call a rat race!

Is it not the game singularly responsible for all the maladies of our times? Why are more people suffering from hypertension? What explains the increasing death toll due to heart attack? Why are our hospitals so overcrowded? Can it be traced to increased aggression in the game of rat race? Can anyone deny that in this race, no holds are barred, that a person is not judged for his inherent worth, but for his ability to work himself into the good books of those who can give him the acceleration he needs to get ahead, to display the ability to bully and browbeat those in the lower rungs of the ladder and send them spinning out of the race, to militantly pursue his self-interest, creating the impression that he alone has the requisite 'initiative'? That track record qualifies the rat race for receiving the rough end of the stick? Yet, it is the game of musical chairs that has come in for attack. Not surprising either. Successful men have an element of gratitude still left in them. They won't go after the rat race, having played that game to gain control over the levers of power. But they need a scapegoat. The game of musical chairs has come in handy. Shed tears, if you have any, for this game that is about to be shown the door in Britain. Thank God, this won't ever happen in India. For the games our leaders play are always around the tunes (music) of *Kissa Kursi* (chairs) *ka*.

Principles and man

The young, by and large, are absolutely sure of themselves. They rush in where angels fear to tread. Ah! You are educated. You are not blind to the implied reference. You know it for what it is, a sly reference that pegs one down as a fool! Tut! Tut! Do you want the young to go after me like a pack of wolves, intent on tearing me to shreds for pillorying them! The young, by and large, are cocksure. What makes the cock so sure? I get a feeling that his certainty springs from the awareness of the fact that he has a brood of hens from amongst whom he can pick his mate at will. He knows that each hen is waiting for him to show his ardour, that they are his to order. If the cock has the will, the hen has the mood. It is this setting that makes the cock so sure. Alas! The fruits of his labour, the eggs, mostly end up as the gourmets' delight. They take myriad shapes and forms, boiled or cooked or roasted, peppered and seasoned, decked in style, further dressed up with *chutney*/sauce and served on plates before the gourmets so that they could play around with spoons and forks and also dine in style. Mercifully, the cock never realises what is happening to the products of his passion. He has no time either. He has fun time, flaunting himself proudly before the hens, strutting around as if he is the crowned king of the brood till, one day, his master decides his head has swelled up with pride and hence, deserves to be placed on the chopping block. The young are cocksure about the correctness of their principles. It is easy for them to do that. They still have not had the experience to see the changing facets of issues relevant to life. Experience is the sum total of one's mistakes. The young have still time to make mistake. Mistakes come in many forms, shapes and sizes. The young go through life, making small mistakes and big mistakes, gigantic slips and gargantuan errors, according to the nature and character of the convictions they uphold, the principles they stick to. They remain stubborn, dare the world to bring a cleavage between the principles they swear by and the expectations of common sense, till they are lashed around, like ships in a storm. Each lash delivers a new experience. The young do not know that experience is the best teacher. By the time, they get that message, they are no longer young. Time kills their cockiness, drives sense into their heads and makes them come round to the view that only Supermen, another word for Mahatmas, can afford the luxury of remaining true to principles and dogmas forever. Others have to give up their principles, tilt with the prevailing winds, save themselves from going down under. The young are no longer young when they learn to handle this shift. Then they see the wisdom in the statement of Groucho Marx, "Those are my principles. If you don't like them I have others."

Crossthoughts

It was the month of June. The sun, blazing at above 40 degrees, and the humidity, aided by a very high sweat factor, pumping out torrents of sweat from every pore of my body, I slumped at the steering, waiting for the policemen, managing what appeared to me a mother of all traffic jams at the ITO crossing, to give the signal to me to drive across.

Minutes ticked by. Still no signal. I felt as if I was being roasted alive. My mood, usually unflappable, heated up and turned me into a rumbling volcano, a fireball of anger. Swear words and invectives flowed out of my mouth. If expletives could have cooled me, I would have turned into frozen ice, instantly. But, alas, every curse only brought in its wake, yet another abuse. I could have easily dictated a dictionary of expletives, if only a recording machine was near at hand.

The horns of vehicles blared. Necks craned out of vehicles to find out what was holding us up. A scooterist, who had wedged himself between my car and the car to my left and been stuck with us, removed the helmet, which acted like as a micro-oven where his bald head was getting grilled, wiped the sweat off his bald pate and face, parked the vehicle, moved to the junction on foot and returned, after sometime, to announce, "No way, sir. Boys are holding a demonstration. The cops are scared to take on the students. Unless the boys end the demonstration, we shall pickle here, for sure."

Suddenly, strange thoughts engulfed me. They showed me the myriad purposes that junctions served.

Is there a better place to hold a demonstration and gain instant publicity for a cause than a trafic junction?

Instant publicity brings to my mind another fact. Ogilvy and his followers saw the immense marketing potential of junctions. They fixed hoardings at major intersections. Here they had a captive audience.

Everyone, who waited at the junction for the signal to turn green killed time by gaping at the hoardings. I think many decisions on buying a new washing machine or a stereo system or any other item, presented by the hoardings in colourful and attractive designs, were taken by quite a few people at one or other of the junctions. The hoardings, alas, roused the ire of our guardian angels, the group of good samaritans who look after safety on roads. They said that the hoardings caused more accidents by diverting the driver's attention. So, the hoardings had to go.

The pleading note of a vendor of dusters, followed by the plaintive appeal of a beggar, hobbling around with the help of a stout pole, gave me yet another insight. The junction is the place where the street vendor makes a living by selling *agarbattis* or dusters or sunshades or slices of coconut; where the beggar who, in some cases, is an expert actor and hobbles as if he has lost a leg or both eyes, makes his fortune.

I heard loud horns from behind, woke up from my trance, found vehicles slowly moving towards the junction, cranked the engine to life, and crawled across the junction after being held up at the crossing for nearly forty minutes, part of which was spent in cerebral exercise, locating the multiple benefits which junctions hold to people.

◆◆◆

On windows

"Windows are the most important tool that's ever been created," Bill Gates. Bill Gates's statement may be seen by many people as a tribute to the window that powers the computer network and lets in free flow of info over the Internet. Alas! they miss the wood for the tree, fail to realise that Bill Gates shaped the window of the computer, structuring it after the conventional window. He wanted it, at our command, to open and let info flow or to shut down and block the flow. What is a window but a 'hole' in the structure, carved out with deliberate care. The architect takes note of which way the wind blows? Does the wind, known for its fickle mind, change direction, with the seasons? If so, what is the wind pattern in the region, round the year? Having done this homework... even the architect has to do a homework. Nobody escapes homework, though we link homework as something that is added on to a student's work-a-day to keep the lad or the lass out of mischief. In July 1998, a minister squirmed because he could not give a convincing reply to questions from the members of the Rajya Sabha. Krishna Kant, the chairman, bailed the minister out saying, "Leave him out. He doesn't seem to have done his homework."... the architect prepares the blue print. He tells the builder, "Here we will have a window. See, it will draw the wind in, take it across the room and let it enter the passage, from where it will reach ... "The architect breaks off to indicate the location of another window, at the end of the passage, through which the wind shall waft out into the open, so that the entire arrangement shall work like an air duct. The builder finds much wisdom in the choice of the right placements of the 'holes'. The architect, having won the builder's approval, adds, "But, you may not like the windows to be always kept open. The waft may be too strong. And, remember, with every waft, a lot of dust too drifts into the house. So, having made the windows, we shall provide shutters. Then, we can have them fully thrown back; or half open; or tightly shut, according to the needs of the time." The builder is beside himself with joy. He savours the power, he has to command the wind. "I let it in, wild and untamed, if I am in a mood to stand such buffeting. Or I control the flow, even cut it off, to suit my taste. Wonderful, my dear architect. You are more powerful than *Vayu Bhagwan*." The shutters of the window are well within reach. So they are, at least in most cases. One can operate them, more easily. No need to get hold of a stool or a chair or a *mooda* to get at the shutters, as is the case when one wants to operate the shutters of ventilators. This friendly attitude of the windows and their shutters makes them my favourite. How I love the window, even though, it is a hole in the structure and hence, an oddity! Behind this love is logic. This logic is easily perceived by anyone forced to stay at home due to indisposition or dislocated joints or other physical infirmities. He realises, in a trice, how lucky he is because he can command a window. I may even add, "Happy is the man who can, at all times, command a crust of bread and a window to sit by and watch the world go by."

Ban the back pocket

AMONG the cases, filed in courts and special courts and superspecial tribunals, to judge alleged acts of omissions and commissions, I do not find any reference to a case against one of the arch criminals of our times. By arch criminal, I have in mind the fashion designer who shifted the pocket, from the front of the shirt, to the rear of the pants, called the new addition, the back pocket or the hip pocket, sang the praise of the innovation and turned on the full power of his *sale-ability* (If the dictionary does not approve of the word, don't be upset. At times, a writer has to find the words to express clearly what is in his mind. 'That is a freedom which the writer enjoys. Not a small freedom, considering that freedom is getting cut down and trimmed by all and sundry) to find enough fans for his new idea. He raised such din and fury that the few sceptics who objected to the back pocket, on the ground that it did not lie in the range of vision of the wearer of the pants and therefore, articles stacked in it might be easily picked by one or other of the members of the gang of nimble fingers, were forced to shut up. The back pocket became the in–thing.

I have a nagging suspicion that the back pocket or the hip pocket... (See, the accursed thing has two names). So it can't be pinned down. It has provided for itself a double image, a dual personality, may be a trick, deftly evolved by some cunning lawyer. Accuse the back pocket and it would wriggle away, saying, "Oh, no, I am the hip pocket. I am wrongly accused." The logic can run in the reverse direction too.), was invented by the fashion designer who worked, hand in gloves, with professional pickpockets.. I even visualise the scenario. The leading light of the pickpockets approached the designer, told him of the hazards faced by his gang while trying to get at the purse or wallet or wad of notes, stacked in the front pocket and offered the designer a fortune if only he could shift the pocket to a location more convenient for the nimble-fingered to operate. Baited by the fat dough, the designer analysed the pants, located, after several sleepless nights, the one place which remains ever outside the watchful eyes of the wearer of the pants. He ended up by moving the pocket to the rear, called it grandly, the *hip pocket*.

He designed the pocket to accept anything with alacrity. He ensured that its 'grabity' (Grab ability. if you want to know what grabity is. Something like earth's gravity, which, really, is a contortion of earth's gravity) knew no limits. It sucks in a fat wallet without the slightest protest. Then it plays Judas. It tells all and sundry, whose eyes hover around the back pocket, that a fortune is waiting to be picked by someone who is daring to play with his deft fingers. It hints to the aspiring pickpocket that he can finish his operation, without the slightest risk. The purse is in the back pocket. The back pocket is out of sight. Anything out of sight is out .of mind, too. For it is no concern of the eyes, what happens at places where they can't reach. The eyes remain blissfully ignorant of what happens out of their range of vision.

This crime.... I mean, being an accomplice to the pickpocket .... is enough to bring the fashion designer to book.

But his crime gets accentuated by the impact of the back pocket on human health. Yes. The back pocket is a health hazard. I have it, on the authority of the American Medical Association that the fashion designer could have been paid fabulous fees by doctors whose practice has multiplied, rapidly, after the move of the pocket to the back. The report of the Medical Association states that persistent sciatica-like pain in the leg and thigh have been noted in chronic carriers of wallets in the back packets. Christening the disease as the Credit Card Syndrome, the Medical Association says the malady can be cured by transplanting the wallet from the back pocket to the breast pocket.

With the twin dangers, listed above .... dangers which go with the title, 'back pocket' .... there is no justification for us to continue to sport the odd contraption on our apparels. The odious design must go. It is making more and more people financial and physical wrecks. How long can we put up with the dangers, just to look in tune with the times? The discordant notes, struck by the back pocket, have, at last, become audible, thanks to the efforts made by the American Medical Association.

It is time the back pocket is banned. It cannot be allowed to play havoc with mankind. It has to be stacked away prominently, among the exhibits of the tools and aids of arch criminals of all times. Ah, what do I hear? The kingpin of the pickpockets wants to make a deal with me, is eager to buy my silence by lining up my purse with fat wads of notes. Who is that man, with that bottle, rippling with urine? The doctor who wants me to keep mum over the harmful effects of the back pocket, the doctor who has come as a representative of the practitioner, who are scared that they will lose much of their income, once patients with sciatica-like pain don't turn up for treatment at their clinics?

Shall I speak out against the back pocket? Or shall I enrich myself and let the back pocket stay, exposing the society to the dangers caused by the back pocket? I have not vacillated, like Hamlet. The back pocket must go. I, for one, am in favour of health. After all, 'health is wealth'. Ban the back pocket. Good health and the back Pocket can't co-exist. That is the moral of the tale.

There is nothing to match the tyranny of adages. They pose as if they are the containers of the essence of human wisdom, declare loudly that one can ignore them only at great peril, and incidentally, rip the shroud of wisdom off one of their own tribe—the proverb that glorifies silence as golden and allocates a secondary position to speech.

It is surprising that this adage is still popular, though, as John Wanamaker rightly observed, 'always and everywhere, the man who speaks well is the man who has the power.'

We hail Socrates as a great philosopher because he had, in addition to an analytical mind, the gift of the gab. He roused the youth of Athens out of the mire of ignorance with his probing questions and prying queries. He fired their desire to search for the Truth, encouraged them to develop the capacity to put to test even dogmas and theories held sacred and sacrosanct and, hence, beyond the realm of sense, enshrined as doctrines which should be accepted, as axioms.

Lord Buddha found enlightenment and cooed like the lark, winning converts to his cause by his preachings. He went round, gathering thousands of followers, exhorting them to give wide currency to the Truth which he had seen, the Truth which he put forth as the panacea to human suffering.

Jesus Christ exploited his power of speech to spread

his message to humanity.

Abraham Lincoln scaled great heights as a national leader and a humanist by allowing his tongue to wag eloquently on the need to cultivate charity, to eschew malice. Sir Winston Churchill transmuted the determination, which coursed through him, save England from the Nazi threat by his stirring appeal to his countrymen to fight against all odds, to resist the enemy at all costs, to carry the struggle on to the plains and over to the hills, beyond the land into the high seas and the air. India began her tryst with destiny with the inspiring call from Pandit Nehru.

History conclusively proves that success and speech are intricately wound together. Only those, who ignore the old proverb that praises silence, foster the potent driving force provided by speech and exploit the immense potentiality of the vocal chord find the golden passport to power, authority, strength and influence.

It is the most vociferous trade union leader who succeeds in getting a better deal for the workers. It is the most loquacious champion of human rights who leaves his imprint on the sands of time.

In short, speech is the very breath of life.

Silence, on the contrary, symbolises death. (That may be the reason why we observe silence in honour of the dead.) It is oppressive, enervating, debilitating. It may be golden, but it evokes in us only the same reaction that swept over King Midas when he touched his dear daughter and found her turned into a beautiful statue of gold.

The most conclusive evidence to sustain the plea that speech is golden comes from America. Charles Dickens, way back in the mid 19th century, toured America, read out his novels before large gatherings and earned sizable fees. Since then, as Wodehouse recorded, every boat that arrives in America brings a swarm of lecturers who are single-minded on one point that there is easy money to be picked up on the lecture platforms of America and they may as well grab it as the next person.

Speech is golden. There is no doubt about it. For, even if you want to counter my contention, you will have to express yourself in words, thus, offering further proof to my conclusion that speech, and not silence, is golden.

The meek do not inherit the earth

One of the axioms that is flaunted around by every Tom, Dick and Harry lauds the meek, indicates that the meek shall inherit the earth.

But, I find, on a fresh look at the axiom, the subtle catch latent in it, the invisible stricture that it passes on the weak and the docile.

It cleverly conceals the fact that men who dare and act, who stake their all for their ideals and strive steadfastedly for reaching their cherished goals, HAVE the earth; they are the men who create noble heritages, bring about technological skill to reap rich harvests of nature's bounty, enrich the world with new ideas and brilliant innovations, alter the quality and content of human life, lead mankind further up the ladder of progress.

The meek wait patiently, biting their fingers or nibbling at their nails, hovering around the periphery, ready to savour the inheritance, as and when it comes to them. And, perhaps, as a wag quipped, when the time comes for the meek to inherit the earth, the inheritance tax will be so high, they won't want it.

It is not surprising that the meek ony wait. That is all what they know. There is no drive in them, no desire to do or die for what hold them in trances, no strength to grapple with the pulls and drags that inevitably face men of action. They live in a world of their own. They follow the philosophy of Tennyson's Lotus Eaters and repeat parrot-like,

'Death is the end of life,

Why should life all labour be?'

What are the achievements of the meek? I can spot none.

Yet, I am wrong. There is one achievement for which the meek deserve full credit. They have coined the slogan, `The meek shall inherit the earth.' That is their only contribution to human thought. Even that is not a direct contribution. The indolence and inertia of the meek must have sparked off the comment from some man of action.

I am sure it was not a meek man who first came down from the trees and tried to take tentative steps on terra firma, stood up on his legs, rather precariously, mastered the art of maintaining his balance, left behind the vestiges of the primordial ape. It was a daring individual who experimented with stone to carve out sharp instruments to hunt animals, who raised a fire by rubbing a stone against stone, and tasted the delicacy of cooked food. It was not a retiring person who dared the high seas on papyrus or reed or wooden rafts, crossed the high seas, made contact with other people, other races. It was a man of action who dreamt of soaring into space; another who made tentative probes with inflated balloons; yet another who added auto engines to steel frames and finally came up with the aeroplane. More recently, a band of daring, dedicated men have given sum and substance to the hopes of man to break the shackles of gravity and to reach out into the stellar universe.

The thrills and excitements of life are reserved for the men who are ambitious, domineering, dynamic and active. The world owes its all to them. They make our earth a better place to live in. They bring about developments in all fields of human activities.

The meek, on the contrary, lead a sedate, steady life. There are no high moments in their lives, no flashes of delight that spring from success against odds. Their lives lack the lustre and glisten that ought to form an integral part of human existence.

They only linger on, waiting for the inheritance. It would be fun to watch how long the meek can keep the earth after they inherit it. (If at all they inherit it!).

The meek, the proverb says, shall inherit the earth.

Quite true. They only inherit. They don't create an inheritance. They don't enrich human thought, add to the sum total of human progress. They don't flex their muscles or exercise their brains. They allow the natural gifts of God to wither away due to disuse, become more weak and fragile, unfit even to hold the inheritance, even if they manage to get it.

All of which lead me to the only conclusion, the meek are weak, and hence, no better than parasites.

Bridges: Concrete and conceptual

THE very mention of bridges—even bridges of understanding—rouses my darkest fears. It creates in me the same emotions which the red rag churns up in a bull. It reminds me of the close link between bridges and double-dealers who are out to fan their interests at the cost of the nation and society.

Bridges subserve the interests of people who have axes to grind. Anyone who talks of building bridges, concrete or conceptual, has his eyes on the profits which he can reap by propagating the need to raise bridges. Either he is in the building trade—a contractor, an engineer, a designer, a steel fabricator, a concrete setter—and is out to make quick money by playing with the mixture of cement and sand, by tinkering with the amount of steel that ought to go into the structure to make it strong and lasting. Or, he is an aspirant in the field of politics and wants to wriggle himself into the good books of the masses before he gains levers of power and makes hay while the power lasts. These are the two distinct categories of people who talk of the need to build bridges to span rivers or hearts. None else.

A cursory look at history brings to us a rare insight. None of the great kings of yore is credited with building bridges. He laid roads. He improved irrigation facilities. He dug wells. He revamped the revenue administration and legal codes. However, he never bothered to build bridges. He kept bridges at arm's length. He knew that dating bridges would be risky. He did not want to burn his fingers by allowing public funds to be swindled by selfseeking builders.

The common man, since time immemorial, never bothered much about bridges. The daring swam across rivers, even when in spate. The less daring resorted to ingenuity. They paddled across in crude native boats, some of them made of bamboo. Or, they cut down a tree to span the two banks of the river so that they could walk across nimbly. Laying a 'pucca' bridge with stone and mortar did not appeal to them.

Without bridges, they felt safe and secure. No enemy could sneak in, undetected. The river provided a natural protective barrier. No girl from the village could be abducted by her paramour from outside the clan. No cultural pollution could happen.

All of which gives me the impression that bridges and we do not mix well with each other.

Once, we realise this basic fact, we are in a much better position to understand why bridges crack and crinkle and collapse much before their estimated life span. (Remember what happened at Goa, a few years back. I even know of a case where a bridge was never built even though official files showed that it had been constructed and the cost duly accounted for.) Kickbacks, hush money, bribes, visible and invisible, deals under the table, (as if the table has eyes on the top, and hence, would become an eyewitness to the crime if the exchange takes place above the table), are some of the reasons why bridges, even when built with steel and cement, come down like houses of cards.

Bridges of understanding too elude us. For we are singularly incapable of demolishing the prejudices of caste or creed or community or religion or region or language. At best, we wear a cloak of understanding over our prejudices; so the bridges of understanding we build lack strength and vigour.

In India, bridges—concrete or conceptual—are built on loose foundations with sub-standard material. For we do not take to bridges like fish to water. Bridges are alien to Indian culture. So they fail to take roots and flourish.

Anyone who talks of bridges has an axe to grind. This realisation makes me shout, "Better no bridges than let self-seekers grind their axes."

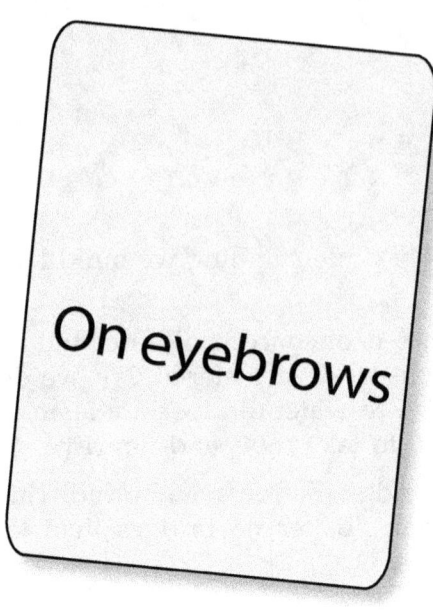

On eyebrows

Try as I do, I fail to realise the purpose behind God's gift of eyebrows to man. Till recently, I clung to the belief that the eyebrows provided a sort of roof over the eyes, so that dust particles, which dart around in the atmosphere, do not find the retina, the right place to land.

But, this conviction has gone with the winds because women, these days, having found the eyebrows real eyesores, shave them off or pluck them out, and insert, in their place, neatly etched lines, carved out by sharpened eyeshadow pencils. Thus have Eves struck a blow against one of God's gift to human beings. Thus have they proved that they are not scared of dust which may end up in their eyes, so long as they have eyelids which know when to wink and when to blink and when to shut. They have given the eyebrows a real beating.

In the process, they have left the ability to raise one's eyebrows, quizzically, to men and old-world women. It is time they realise that the artificial arches, which add to the beauty of their eyes, do not perform this task efficiently. It needs hair to bristle and throb and flutter with every raise of the eyebrows to make the exercise worth the efforts. Sans the hair, the eyebrows look arid like the desert, lifeless and listless.

Those who raise their eyebrows, questioning this comment, are the very women who have modernised the settings of their eyes. For them, the wide range of signals, which one can send through the tilt and angle and bend and stretch of the eyebrows shall ever ramain out of reach.

Now that a large section of humanity has chosen to do away with natural eyebrows—one wonders whether the theory of evolution, so grandly defined by Charles Darwin, shall operate and slowly, but steadily, put the eyebrows out of existence, though this may take several centuries. . . the eyebrows are facing tough times. The death knell is ringing the sounds with all the dismal notes it can strike. The rings carry the message, "For whom the bell tolls? For the eyebrows."

However, eyebrows are not affected by such eerie notes. They know that humans are not the only species to which they can cling on. In fact, even inanimate objects have started courting eyebrows with enthusiasm. And some of them are learning how to raise the eyebrows to get the maximum impact.

Ah! that leaves a trail of questioning notes, all around, some accompanied by raising of real eyebrows, some of shady eyebrows with all the shadiness which go with false facades, about my sanity. How could inanimate objects arm themselves with eyebrows?

Bear with me, for a second, and the reason will become evident, right away. I have a report in this eveninger, to which I turn as dusk falls, to fill up the gaps in my knowledge since I read the morning newspaper. There it is, an interesting report, which tells me that newspapers have started raising their eyebrows, in no uncertain terms. Here is the report for you to cull, "The frolicking antics of the younger members of the British Royalty, when the country's forces are engaged in a grim battle with the Iraqis, have made British papers raise their eyebrows in no uncertain terms."

One may go along with Lewis Carrol, take a dip into the wonderland through which Alice took a trip, yet fail to find eyebrows on newspapers. Alice... poor girl... had to slide down the hole and travel through the strange land to get wierd experiences. We, having shifted eyebrows, from the anatomy of modern dames, to newspapers, for a start are preparing a veritable wonderland around our normal settings. Alice may raise her eyebrows, in no uncertain terms, but she may shy away when some modern Eve tells Alice, she is out of date, obsolete, behind the times when she goes around, holding on to eyebrows.

Y EAR after year, around this time, I get a touch of Hamlet. A great dilemma, very much in the style of the Prince who debated, with all the earnestness at his command, on whether to be or not to be, nabs me.

This dilemma starts with the arrival of a few diaries, which are handed over to me by friends, who have access to them, who after keeping a few, which are the best among the lot for themselves, palm off those diaries for which they find no earthly use on friends and acquaintances.

The sight of half-a-dozen diaries, of various shapes and sizes, makes me a little unsure of myself. I begin to wonder whether I shall remain blind to the virgin charms of the diaries, each one parading itself before me with only one thought in mind. I do not miss the message. Each one wants me to take it on, pour out may creative thoughts into it, make it the repository of the secrets which I do not want to share with anyone.

Collectively, they are willing to serve me, be my own, in every way, to do as I like. They shall not demur if I show a preference to one of them. I can have a harem of diaries, rule over the harem, dictatorially, turn away, once my passion is stilled, from one to date another, behave like a butterfly that flirts around, pollinating every flower within reach, yet refusing to stay true to any one of them. Such blind adoration, I never receive from any human being.

That is where the diaries pep up my spirits, convey to me the feeling that while I may not be the Prince Charming to the fair sex, these diaries do look upon me as the most handsome man this side of Suez.

The open invitation to deflower them does make me waver. I flounder, pout my lips. (Someone points out that I can never be the top pouter, till I master the art by taking a few lessons from India's one-time Prime Minister, Late Mr. Narasimha Rao. He adds that every pouter is basically a Hamlet. For, doubts, indecisiveness, waverings are the hallmarks of the royal pouter.) Then began a debate about a wisdom in putting my trust in the diaries.

The doubts get dispelled, soon enough.

The truth dawns, in a trice.

It will be risky to keep a diary.

The reason is not far to seek.

One expects a diarist to be brutally frank, to confide without any gloss or varnish which covers up the truth in vague generalities. Herein lies the real danger.

One instance shall suffice. Can I make an entry, in the diary, about some major failing of my better half, and feel safe? I can keep the diary under lock and key, but, then, where is the lock that is unpickable? Further, if the fair dame, who claims she is my better half, walks in while I am recording a censor of her conduct and snatches the diary, in a trice, reads the entry and whips up a domestic war, I with all the draconian consequences of the hurt which she feels deep within after noticing the disparaging remarks, is there anyway, I can keep the domestic triangle on the square? (Geometricians may find enough scope to pick holes in the suggestion that any triangle can be squared. I shall shy away from them. For I do not want to get entangled in theorems, axioms and corollaries, the essence of geometry which presented enough obstacles in my path during my days at school).

I cannot afford the luxury of being brutally frank and recording truly, without any concern for the danger which shall become a part of my very existence, if and when one or other of the persons, on whose good books, I currently am, gets to know of my real view of his personality and look upon the entry in the style of the bull which sights a red rag. The very thought of the danger gives me the jitters. I shiver, from head to toe, when I sense that if I date the diary, I shall be laying the ground for a new angle of vision. I see the picture (which too is a sort of writing) on the wall. This picture is of a WRECKTANGLE, which has nothing in common with the rectangle, which indicates that the TANGLE shall WRECK my peace of mind, forever.

The diaries... all of them... are thrown away, into the nearest dustbin. At times, the nearest dustbin happens to be a friend or a relative, eager to have a diary, and envy me for the rich collection I hold. At times, it is one or other of the children who finds that sketches and diagrams can find no better place to thrive than on the pages of the diaries.

This has been the pattern, year after year. Thus, have I ensured safety and security. I agree that, at a later date, when someone wants to know how I felt, at a particular moment of my life, about someone or the other, he or she may draw a blank because no private diaries are available. But, then, this is a minor discomfiture which the gang of postmortem experts must put up with. For, I find that every time an eminent man's diaries are made public, (always after his death), his reputation gets chipped as much as of those at whom he had cavilled at during his lifetime, (some of them outlive him and see what he had said about them, mostly not adulatory, by and large critical).

I concede that I am no VIP. Not even a minor one. But who knows what the future has in store for me?

Safety lies in keeping away from a diary. Let me play safe, be true to my pattern of keeping away from diaries, this year too.

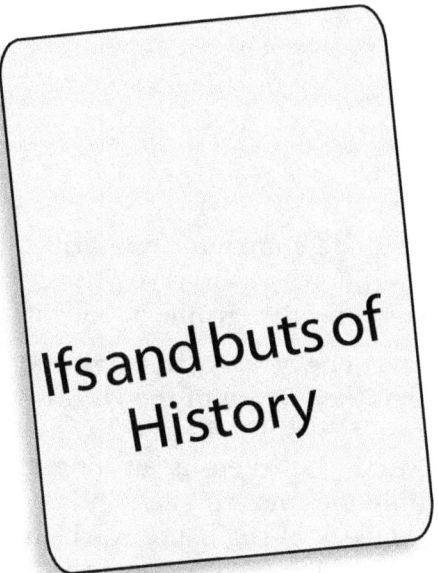

Ifs and buts of History

A CATCHY observation draws me, irresistibly, to the two-letter word—'IF', and makes me realise the immense power it holds. All other words, packed with many more alphabets, are laden with their own different pronunciations. (There is what is known as Queen's English... or King's English, if a King is on the throne of England... which is supposed to set the standards, when it comes to pronunciation). But there are all sorts of variations which each word gains as English is courted by people from various corners of the world. The way a word is pronounced changes even within the substrata of a society. Thus, we know how English words carry the tang of each language group. (That being the case, all long words, which need strings of alphabets, get warped and twisted and thrown out of shape when they are handled by people, who can never get over the distinct slants which are basic to their very existence and which are strongly influenced by the intonations and stresses of the mother tongue of each user). These run the risk of losing their identities, even becoming stranger to themselves, as is the case with the word, PLEASURE, when handled by a *Punjabi* or the word NATION, spoken by a *Bihari*; or the word COLLEGE, which gets a closer approximation to COLLAGE when a Keralite dates it.

It is here that the word, 'IF' stands out. Nobody can ever mispronounce it. If only all the words share this invariant nature of the word, IF, even we can go on the TV network, read the news at prime time without earning any snappy or snide comment from critics like Amita Malik. This, by itself, forces us to give due attention to the word. Then we step on other truths about this word.

Long years ago, someone had the audacity to claim that the history of the world would have taken a different course, if only Cleopatra's nose had been shaped differently. Mind you, there is an infinite range of noses. (There are bulbuous noses, sharp noses, noses which remind us of the beak of eagle, noses which have a flattened look, noses which dominate or noses which carry subservient notes).

Look at every page of history. We find the word, IF, holding court there, drawing our attention to the myriad possibilities which were available to the leading lights of the day. Yet, by a configuration of thoughts, ideas, events, moves, etc., the course of history was nudged along a particular path. IF only King Edward VIII had never run into Wally Simpson, a divorced American dame and found that, among the crores of dames on the face of the earth, in the late '30s, she alone measured up to his concept of beauty and therefore, qualified to be his better-half! IF Lal Bahadur Shastri had not died after signing the Tashkent agreement, IF he had lived for a longer duration and held the office of Prime Minister, would the nation ever have gone through that era of Emergency!

I need not list out more such IFs of history to drive home my point. The power of IF is evident, even to the meanest intelligence. There it stands, this compressed pack of power, this two-letter word, teasing us to predict what the future shall unfold, telling us, in no uncertain terms, that all the suspense and drama of the greatest mystery story of all times shall always take second place to the creative products of this word, with its infinite possibilities and wide ranging uncertainties.

◆◆◆

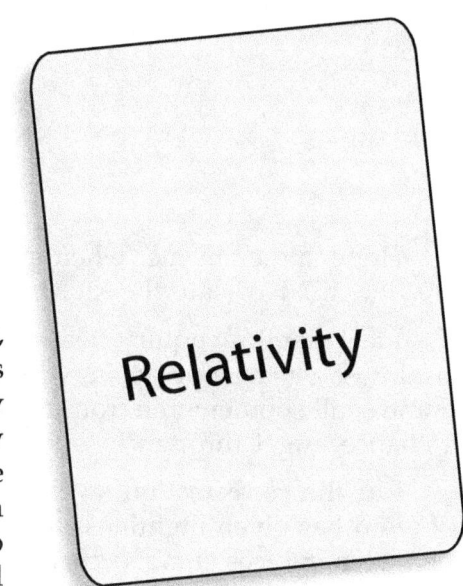

DURING his lifetime, Einstein, the genius who gifted to humanity an insight into the law of relativity, held the view that apart from him, hardly one or two others really understood what it was all about.

In a lighter vein, he pointed out how an hour, with a charming, witty damsel, can seem like a minute, while even a minute, with one's back close to a raging fireplace, can look sixty times longer. In the process, he brought out a unique phenomenon. Time has no intrinsic strength in it. It adjusts to the mood of the individual. It lengthens or contracts, depending on the state of mind of the individual.

It is this message which is conveyed to me, as I wait, hopefully, just across the glass door of the telephone booth. I have an urgent message to convey to a colleague. I want certain clarifications to seek on a matter of prime importance.

Inside the booth is a demure young woman. I watch her profile, through the half-open door. She looks sleek, modern, with the nail-polish flashing red as she casually swings her free hand. The jingles of the bangles turn out an esoteric tune, which, but for my impatience, may have taken me to the heights of delight.

But, I remain immune, not only to the vital statistics of the dame, but even to the lovely notes which the bangles produce. I fidget, restlessly, as the dame keeps on talking. I wonder whether she will talk on till the cows come home. (One doesn't associate cows with city dames. But, an idiom finds the mark, even if the target is a city-bred woman).

Hope surges in me, when she coos, "Ah ... so ... You are fine, hi? How are the kids?..."

I feel that this enquiry clearly indicates that the *gupshup* is almost over. Hope springs in me. I conclude that the dame shall soon emerge from the booth. Then shall I have a chance to get through to my colleague?

But the conversation swings up, as if a sudden gust of wind has given flightiness to the petering conversation. The woman races along, occasionally listening to whatever it is that comes across the line, before offering comments, titbits, giggles, and a lot of OOHS and AHs. I look at my watch. I find that I have been waiting, now, for about ten minutes. But, in my frenzied state, I feel I have been there for ages. I run my palm over my chin to test whether I have grown a beard, in true Rip Van Winkle style, during this interminable wait.

I wonder how I shall get this dame out of the booth. Shall I knock at the glass door, slightly, to indicate that she has already taken an inordinately long time? Shall I just push my way in, forcibly pull the knob and thus, put an end to the connection? I am at my wit's end. Casually, I turn back and see two others, gaping at each other, unsure of when their turn shall come, if it comes at all.

Once again, I hear, "I think I shall now hurry. Has to get back home, before the kids return ...." Once again, hope fills me. But these hopes are dashed, in a second, as the dame remembers some other titillating incident which she has to share with whoever it be at the other end.

At last, after four or five false notes of conclusion, the dame finally decides, she has had her say. She breezes out, ignores my stern stare and glides off, as if her conduct cannot be faulted.

I enter the booth, take my own sweet time to talk to my colleague. I not only refer the matter on hand, but take time to gossip. I do not realise how quickly time flies, as we talk about recent developments, analyse the nature and traits of a new executive, debate plans for a holiday in the hills, during October.

Every time the conversation seems to dip, a fresh idea or a new topic comes up. When I finally put the receiver down, I think I have spent hardly three minutes. But one look at the watch makes me wince; I have been at it for fifteen minutes.

That is a new definition on relativity for you. When you wait for access to the telephone, a minute is as long as an hour; and when you are at the phone, an hour is just as short as a minute.

Critics, authors and artists

NO aspiring author or artist has looked kindly towards the critics who 'are sentinels in a grand army of letters, stationed at the corners of newspapers and reviews to challenge every new author'. That explains all the caustic remarks made about critics. A wag quipped that a critic is 'a person who would have you write it, sing it; play it or paint it as he would do it if he could.' Oliver Wendell. Holmes sneered at the critics with the words, 'What a blessed thing it is that nature, when she invented, manufactured and patterned her artists, contrived to make critics of the chips that were left'. Dale Carnegie noted, 'Any fool can criticise, condemn and compliment; and most fools do.'

It cannot be denied, however, that critics have a valuable role to play in separating the chaff from the grain, in exposing the weaknesses of an artist so that he might put in an extra effort to overcome them, in keeping the artist ever on his toes.

But, there are critics and critics. I find that the critical comments of those who have a real flare for the task have a flavour that lingers on forever. Reviewing the play, "LADDER", George Kaufmann said, "I saw it under adverse condition. The curtain was up:"

Equally telling is the comment, a critic made about another play, "Curtain rose on his performance at 6.30. Audience rose at 6.35." How stunning is the critical remark, "The programme started at 6 p.m. sharp and ended at 9 p.m. dull." Christopher Fry, after enduing a laborious play, said, 'Oh, his pauses are no longer pregnant; they are in labour.'

John Steinbeck reviewed the film, SAMSON AND DELILAH : 'Saw the movie; loved the book.' Noel Coward said about a play, 'In this play, two things need to be cut. One: the third act; and two: the singer's throat.' Brook Atkinson, after seeing the play, 'HALF WAY TO HELL, commented. 'When the author calls his play, HALF WAY TO HELL, he underestimates the distance.' David Lardner observed about an over-rated comedy, 'The plot was designed in a light vein which speedily became varicose.'

An actress who put up a poor show got the shock of her life when she read the criticism, 'What an actress! Even if she were cast as Lady Godiva, the horse would steal the show.' A critic explained why Rome burnt while Nero fiddled; 'If Nero played fiddle the way this fellow does, no wonder they burned Rome.'

After listening to a bad performance of a lady singer, the critic could not resist the temptation to snipe at her: 'Her singing was mutiny on the high Cs.' A critic, reviewing THE DIRTIEST SHOW IN TOWN, which ran to packed houses in London in January and February 1973, said, 'It is.'

I particularly relish some gems of critical thoughts from the world of books. Samuel Johnson dismissed Gray's ODES as 'cucumbers'. He added, `Gray has a kind of strutting dignity and is tall by walking on tiptoe.' Speaking about another author, Johnson said, 'That fellow, Richardson, on the contrary, could not be content to sail quietly down the stream of reputation without longing to taste the froth from every stroke of the oar.' About another author, Johnson growled, 'He treads upon the brink of a meaning.'

One of the most delectable criticism was made on the book, 'ZULFIE, MY FRIEND' by Pilloo Mody. The critic noted, 'What a heavyweight author; what a lightweight book!' When Lord Chamberlain wrote his biography, 'LORD CHAMBERLAIN REGRETS', pat came the critical comment, 'For once, we agree with his Lordship.' Mr Attlee called his autobiography, 'AS IT HAPPENED' and inadvertently, provided Mr Bevan the chance to have a dig at him. Tongue-in-cheek, Mr Bevan commented, "It's a good title. Things happened to him. He never did anything."

Caught on the wrong foot

The tongue is mightier than the sword. The thrusts and parries and wounds that the tongue can deliver often outweigh the deft blows that the sword can deliver. When the replies to innocent questions strike back with venom, the recepient is left tongue-tied, disgraced and virtually de-based and helpless.

The patient who asked the doctor, "How can I avoid falling hair?" would not have anticipated, even in his wildest dreams, that he would get the answer, "Jump out of the way."

It is a general tendency to remark, when introduced to someone, "Have not I seen your face somewhere?" This innocuous statement may get you a snub. The new acquaintance may well say, "No. It has always been where it is now". You have no other alternative except to put on a broad grin to conceal your chagrin.

A woman emigrated to the United States. On arrival, she was asked by officials, "Do you advocate the overthrow of the Government of the United States of America by subversion or violence? "The woman tossed the problem in her mind for sometime and quietly muttered, "Violence."

The postal clerk weighed a letter and told the sender, "It is heavy. You will have to put a fifteen paise stamp on it in addition to the stamps affixed by you." The sender spluttered, "What! That will make it even heavier."

On spotting a fly in the cup of coffee brought by the waiter; a man complained, "See. This fly has found a place in the coffee." The waiter smiled enigmatically and replied, "Ssh. Everybody will want one."

A woman visitor to the zoo asked the keeper, "Is this hippopotamus a male or a female?" The keeper had no qualms in giving a reply. He said, "Madam. That is a question that should be of interest to another hippopotamus."

The experience of an income tax official makes interesting reading. He was sitting in his office, comfortably scrutinising the figures submitted by the tax payers, when a tax payer entered. The official stared at the tax payer and spotted the adhesive tapes which crossed the bridge of the nose of the tax payer. The official enquired politely, "Had an accident to your nose?" The retort was stunning, "Oh, I have been paying trough my nose for so long that my nose caved in under the strain." The official had no comments to make.

I recollect an instance when Mrs. Renu Chakravarty was floored by Pandit Pant. The occasion was the debate on the law and order situation in Kerala during the communist regime in 1958-59. Mrs. Chakravarty interrupted Mr. Pant and raised a point of objection. Pandit Pant ignored her querry. The member persisted. "What about the point raised by me?" she thundered.

The Home Minister did not hesitate for a second. He responded immediately, "Your point is like the point in geometry without length, breadth and depth."

Once Sheridan made a virulent attack against a member of Parliament. The Speaker moved in and insisted that the criticism was venomous and that Sheridan should apologise. Sheridan rose in his seat, bowed and added, "Mr. Speaker. I said the honourable member was a liar, it is true and I am sorry for it. The honourable member may insert the punctuation marks where he pleases."

It was a hot day. Lawrence of Arabia was standing in the porch of a Cairo hotel. A woman, anxious to be seen in his company approached him. "Imagine, Col. Lawrence. Ninety-two already. "She fanned herself and commented on the heat. "Indeed," Col. Lawrence replied, "Congratulations, Madam, and many happy returns of the day." The lady disappeared as if hit by a storm.

Equally disastrous was the experience of a lady who spotted W. C. Fields and walked over to his side. She smiled and asked, "Do you believe in clubs for women?" With a twinkle in his eyes, Fields replied, "Yes. I do." He paused and added, "If every other form of persuasion fails."

A doctor advised Sydney Smith that it would be good to take a walk on an empty stomach. Smith retorted, "Whose?" On another occasion, Smith was involved in a heated argument with a county squire. The squire shouted angrily, "If I had a son who was an idiot, by jove, I'd make him a parson." This was a dig at Smith who was a parson. Smith smiled and said in a clear voice, "Very probably. But, I see that your father was of a different mind."

But, the best among such jokes must be attributed to a student who was instructed by his teacher to write a story involving surprise, sex, royalty and mystery. Little did he expect the story that the student wrote glibly and passed on to him. The story was short and crisp. It read—"What! Pregnant again!" asked the princess of her maid. The maid replied, "Do not know how it happened."

Brevity, certainly, is the soul of wit.

◆◆◆

AMONG the most illogical posters of the world—and I can tell you that when it comes to logic, many posters fall flat—pride of place must be given to the one which I notice, stuck to iron gates of many posh buildings.

In simple English, it holds out a warning to dogs, if only they could read, which tell them that the terrain which lies beyond the gates is a forbidden territory, that if they trespass, they would face dire consequences.

By some convoluted logic, of which only man is capable, the poster has gained an absurd connotation. The poster is a warning, not to dogs but to human beings to keep away from the area. The message is meant to warn anyone who thinks of getting in that half-a-dozen snarling, furious, froth-ing dogs shall set upon him, in a trice, and drive their sharp teeth into any part of his body. By the time, the victim wriggles himself out of the bloody mess, he may present an ungainly sight. And he may not have the strength to argue, "But, this poster does not say 'BEWARE OF DOGS.' Then I would have kept away. But this poster says, 'DOGS BEWARE' .... Tut... Tut."

That catchy caption, we, who have had close encounters of the type described above, know, is not meant to warn dogs, but humans. The poster may be inconsistent with the basics of the English language. But who cares?

Some intelligent humans have now taken to this poster, even when they have no dogs as pets. The other day, I decided to call at a friend's place. I found the big board, which said, 'DOGS BEWARE'. I hesitated, at the gates. I peeped, carefully, to spot the dogs which I expected to come charging. I waited, before pressing the calling bell. Still no dogs appeared on the scene, yelping or barking. The whole situation was puzzling.

Finally, I gathered all the courage which I could muster, opened one of the gates, ever so slightly, ready to ram it shut after retreating if any dog made a dash for me. But, no dog sprang out of the drive-in. No dog spoiled the scene with its gory presence. Instead, I spotted my friend, standing on the *verandah*, giving me a welcome smile. I asked him, "Where, Oh, where are your dogs?"

The question took him by surprise. Then he saw light. He grinned, "Dogs? I don't have any dog around." I pointed to the poster, stuck to one of the gates. He then clarified, "Ah, that's to keep beggars, unwanted salesmen and mischievous children out."

While I was still trying to see the cleverness of my friend, I had another experience, which provided me with yet another insight into the subtle meaning that the poster often presents.

I decided to drop in at my aunt's place. I parked the car, walked up to the gate. My eyes riveted on the poster, 'DOGS BEWARE'. I felt a little upset. For, my aunt, well past middle age, had never shown an inclination to date pups and dogs. Before I could conclude that she too had taken the board, out of a belief that the poster would keep beggars, salesmen and urchins away, a small pet, making infantile squeaks, ran up to the gate. It whelped, raised itself on its hind legs, as if ready to drive fear into me. Its antics looked so harmless that I almost burst out laughing.

That was when my aunt, her silvery hair, tied neatly in the shape of a bun at the nape of her neck, waddled up to the gate, took time to identify me, and then told me, "Come in, Kichu... But take care. Don't step on my *Chihuahua*. It is so small that if you step on it, it will be turned into pulp. That is why I put up that board!"

The thumb, described by Chambers dictionary as 'the short, thick digit, consisting of two phalanges, on the radial side of the human hand' has, at last, been accorded its rightful place in the  Indian Parliament. On August 2, 1978, the Speaker of the Lok Sabha, Mr Hegde, after considering a complaint by the Hon'ble.—H. L. Patwari, decreed that the show of thumbs was parliamentary.

The Speaker (I consider the name a misnomer)—It is the Speaker who speaks the least. Yet he is called the Speaker while all others who rave and rant, go into tantrums, reveal their flare for words, do not qualify for the honour)—has thus removed one major cause of complaint, which many members who had mastered the technique of exploiting their thumbs to drive home their points, had been nurturing for long.

No longer will the prancing, dancing thumb, handled expertly by an Hon'ble Member of the Lok Sabha, earn him an icy stare from the Chair. Ah, don't ask me how the Chair can stare. The Chair, here, stand's for the Speaker. All very confusing, I agree. Other Hon'ble Ministers and Members too are occupying chairs, but it is the Speaker who gets recognition and is identified with the Chair. The Speaker seems to have all the benefits when it comes to titles and names.

Nor will the Speaker breathe down the nape of the member who, finding words ineffective to express the feelings which surge within him, sports his thumb to wrest the advantage. Instead, the Speaker will turn a blind eye, if not a pair of blind eyes. Or, if he is in no mood to turn blind eyes to what is happening in the House, he may watch the oscillations of the thumb with utmost unconcern, let out a few yawns and lean further back in the chair. (That will be truly a case of a Chair leaning on a chair. A very amusing proposition, indeed).

When inclined to enjoy the revelries, the Speaker may even go into ecstasy, watch the antics of the thumb, and wish that he too could give the liberty to his thumb to perform any dance, even a tap dance.

The thumb, thus, will provide much-needed diversion in the House. Its performance will take away the sting in the charges that the Hon'ble Members hurl at each other. Its acts will suck out the rage and ire which mark many of the debates in Parliament. Thus, the thumb will make the Lok Sabha a much better place to work. Consequently, the business of managing the affairs of the State will become smoother, easier and, hence, better.

These facts weigh with me when I dwell on the freedom accorded to the Hon'ble Members of our Lok Sabha to turn to their thumbs when words fail them. It can now be asserted that the thumb has come 'thumbs up'.

The triumph of the thumb, after more than 30 years of bondage, is a historic event. It is as momentous as August 15, 1947, when India began the Tryst With Destiny. This tryst began on a right note, but one elementary freedom—the freedom to exploit the thumb—had failed to find a place in our August Constitution. It did not form part of our fundamental rights.

The wrong has been righted now. The freedom. accorded to the thumb to swing and to caper in the Lok Sabha, adds a new dimension to Indian democracy. One more fetter, which had corroded the essence of freedom, has been broken.

It can be asserted with certitude that August 2, 1978, is bound to be remembered till eternity, at least by those who love their thumbs. I think it would be in the fitness of things to designate August 2 as the 'Day of the Thumb'. Every year the Day of the Thumb may be celebrated with due propriety by the votaries of the thumb.

The thumb is what sees us through life.

When we are just tiny babies, lying flat on our backs, knowing not any other pleasure than the one that springs from sucking at the mammary glands of our mothers, we, perforce, turn to the thumb to fill in the void when we find the mammary glands not readily available.

From then on, we grow with the realisation that there is no existence without the thumb. We can't hold a pencil without the help of the thumb. Or for that matter, a spoon or a plate or an arrow on the bow.

The value pitched on the thumb can be gauged by the fact that Dronacharya demanded the thumb of Ekalavya as *Gurudakshina*. Ekalavya obliged. He knew that Dronacharya, whom he had accepted as his Guru, had asked the unusual fees because the Guru was afraid that Ekalavya would turn out to be a much better at archery than Arjuna. Without the thumb, Ekalvya realsied that he could never be an archer. Dronacharya played a dirty trick on poor Ekalavya.

We would all be like Ekalvya if we are left to fend for ourselves, sans the thumbs.

How will modern, lovely lissom college girls get free lifts if they can't wave their thumbs at fast-moving vehicles, indicating their desire to join the ride? Many artists who made a name for themselves by drawing thumb-nail sketches will find themselves on doles if they have to face the world without their thumbs. The cop, when out to extract confession from a hardened criminal, turns to the thumbscrew with alacrity and gets the desired result.

That explains, in brief, the role that the thumb plays in human life.

I hear someone say that there was a little boy who put in his thumb and pulled out a plum. I also overhear him comparing me with the little boy, stating that I have put an envelope, containing this treatise on the thumb, through the slit in the letter box of the Press by holding it delicately between my thumb and my index finger and pulled out a plum, a fat cheque from the Editor.

'Thumbs Up' is all that I can do. And none can accuse me of doing something that is unparliamentary.

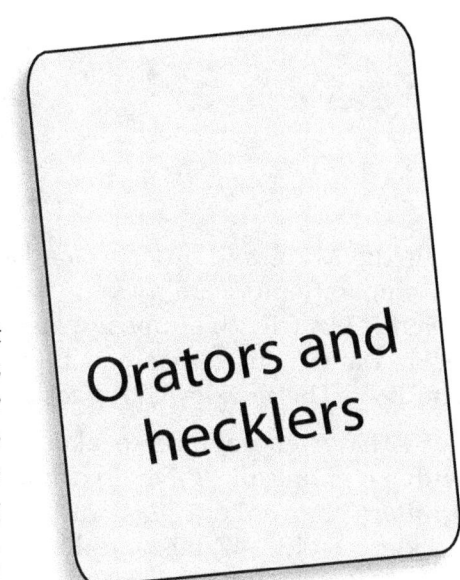

Orators and hecklers

Despite the fact that eminent speakers usually get the better of hecklers, these intruding voices have not lost hope of getting the better of the orators. Their tenacity is indeed remarkable. And it is this consistency that wins them the occasional laurels which have brought many a silver-tongued rambler tumbling down.

When William Jennings Bryan bombastically said, "I wish I had the wings of a bird to fly to every village and hamlet in America to tell you people about this question," a heckler interjected. "You'd be shot for a goose before you had flown a mile."

Once Dale Baughman was explaining to an audience his background and early childhood in Brown county, Indiana. He said, "Now, I wasn't born in a log cabin, but my folks moved into one just as soon as they could afford it. I started out in life as a bare-footed boy." Just then a voice from the rear cut through the hall, "Brother, none of us was born with shoes on."

A candidate for the U.S. Congress finished his oration with the words, "In conclusion, I wish to state that I was born a Democrat, have always been a Democrat and expect to die a Democrat". That provoked a heckler to quip, "Not very ambitious, are you?"

Theodore Roosevelt was continuously interrupted by a heckler who went on shouting, "I'm a Democrat." Roosevelt paused and then addressed the heckler: "May I ask the gentleman why he is a Democrat?" The intruder replied: "My grandfather was a Democrat, my father was a Democrat, and I am a Democrat." Roosevelt smiled and asked, "My friend, suppose your grandfather had been a jackass and your father had been a jackass, what would you be?" The heckler shot back, "A Republican".

A lady temperance speaker concluded her peroration with a clarion call, "Give up drinks. I would rather commit adultery than take a glass of beer." Immediately, came a heckler's voice, "Who wouldn't?"

A young barrister was a candidate from a Lok Sabha constituency in Gujarat. He said, "I'm very pleased to address this working class constituency. It may interest you to know that I'm a working man myself. In fact, I often work when you are asleep". That was enough to trigger the heckler who spat out, "You must be a blooming burglar."

During the election campaign in Britain, a Labour Party candidate asked rhetorically, "Why have we the finest generation of children ever known in this country?" The candidate hoped to stress the social welfare schemes that the Labour Party had in mind. But he got a big shock when a heckler shouted, "Because they were produced by private enterprise."

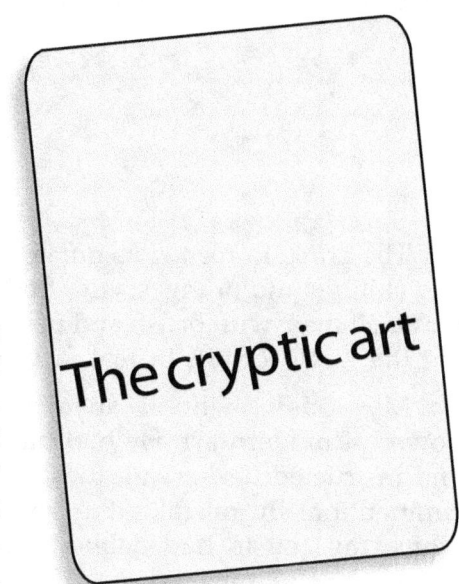

The cryptic art

ART, it is said, lies in concealing art: Judged by this standard, modern art is the most perfect art. It never reveals its true meaning and purpose. Instead, it takes refuge behind a conglomeration of intricate patterns and challenges us to unravel its mystery. That is why my blood pressure shoots up when people eulogise modern art for its enigmatic beauty and cryptic grace.

Gone, indeed, are the days when a rose painted on a canvas resembled a rose. What we get today is a combination of cubes and squares arranged in disorder and filled up with all sorts of colours to create an impression of anything but the flower that it purports to represent.

The portrait of a graceful damsel is cleverly distorted by modern art to disappear into a few vertical and horizontal lines. These paintings with their splash of colours fail to rouse our emotion or fan our artistic senses.

Why, then, do we go about praising modern art? Mainly because it has become a fashion with us to patronise modern art. Most of us are afraid that we would be dubbed old fashioned if we did not get into ecstatic moods when discussing modern art.

In an effort to impress others, we go into raptures and allow our vocal chords to articulate eulogies on modern art. Unable to understand the meaning of the painting, we toe the line of safety by applauding the artist for his exceptional talent.

The artist, in turn, gets inflated ideas of his importance and abilities and plunges, with fresh vigour, into the studio, playing havoc with brush and paint. He thinks he is enriching the world of art. In real fact, he only confounds us.

My cousin, who is an artist, confirms the mystic power of modern art. He had painted the scene of sunset and instructed his servant to post it to the organisers of a competition. By mistake, the servant mailed a canvas on which my cousin had dabbed the excess paint from the brushes.—The mistake was detected only after the last date for entries. My cousin threw up his hands in disgust and scolded the servant for the mistake. It, therefore, came to him as a great surprise when his entry was adjudged the best.

On another occasion, he had sent a painting for an art exhibition. To his utter consternation, not a soul gave a second glance to the lifelike painting of a horse. He was so disheartened that he turned the painting upside down when nobody was present.—Lo! the painting became the centre of attraction. Men and women stood before it, fascinated by the intricate charm and vitality of the painting. Since this event, my cousin has been taking a topsy-turvy view of life. Poor chap! You cannot blame him for practising *Shirsasan* while painting.

The other day, I overheard a couple of ladies leaving an art exhibition.

"Abstract paintings. I can't have them in my house," one lady said decisively. "After all, I've a sixteen-year-old daughter."

"What has that got to do with. . ."

"Well," the first lady cut her short, "with those abstract paintings, you never know whether they are decent or not."

THERE HAS appeared in the market a new type of watch which winds itself with the slightest movement of the hand.

You are lured into purchase by the suave, persuasive language of the dealer, who is adept in painting a glorious picture of the new contraption. He assures you that the possession of the watch would free you from the botheration of winding. He reveals the truth that you save five minutes daily, thirty hours every year. With much gusto, he rallies the final figure: you save one hundred and twenty man-days in the whole lifetime.

He appeals to your patriotism by pointing out the colossal waste of man-power because the 500 million people of India are still without the automatic watch.

His arguments carry the day and you buy the self-winding mechanism with great delight.

You are elated when you wear the watch on your left wrist. You recollect that the watch gains its life from the movement of your left hand.

Then you realise, suddenly, that your left hand is absolutely immobile! Every other part of your body is in eternal motion, but not your left hand which sticks to its vertical posture and refuses to budge.

You look down at the hand with frustration. Anger sweeps over you. You get a nagging doubt that the left hand is least inclined to cooperate; that it is jealous of the new watch and is trying to stifle its spark.

The watch is running down, slowly. And it will die unless the left hand obliges. This realisation makes you restless.

You decide to make the left hand act according to your dictates. You swing the hand viciously in all directions till it creeks with pain and threatens to get dislodged itself from the shoulder. You perform physical exercises and *asans*, raise the left hand to impossible angles, and repeat the performance till the hand has no more life in it.

Your attitude undergoes a radical change with the possession of the watch. You evince a fresh vigour and zest when you shake hands with your friends. You grab the outstretched hand of the friend with both hands and shake it for a long time. When you converse, you bring your left hand into use, gesticulating with much enthusiasm that was lacking before the watch got on to your wrist.

Brushing the teeth, which was the prerogative of the right hand, now becomes the duty of your left hand. You spend more time in brushing the teeth which gain a lustre that transforms your personality. Shoe-shining (your own shoes) becomes your pet hobby. You are ready to help in domestic chores that promise enough motion for the left hand, replenishing the energy pack of the automatic watch.

True. You are free from the botheration of winding the watch. But you pay the penalty in the form of strict watch over the left hand. You undergo excessive strain to keep the hand in motion.

Do I hear someone shouting: "Those grapes are sour?" Quite correct. I do not have an automatic watch.

Symbol of gratitude

IT WAS Pascal, the great French thinker, who said, "The more I see of men, the more I like dogs. "It was his firm view that the dog was the perfect symbol of gratitude, a trait conspicuously absent in human beings. Perhaps, man does not practise this virtue because, unlike the dog, he has no tail to wag. What an advantage the dog has over man!

But one has to draw a line between one's own dog and another man's dog. The neighbour's dog invariably takes an attitude of hostility to you. It eyes you with suspicion when you take a stroll in the small garden of your house. When you approach the thorny hedge which stands like a protecting deity, the dog gives you an icy stare and howls viciously as if it wants its voice to reach the UN headquarters, registering a case of aggression against you.

A few more steps closer to the hedge and the dog throws aside all canons of man-beast relationship. It pounces on you, depriving you of a few pounds of flesh which may come from any part of your body: the dog does not care. It wants its pounds of flesh, nothing more, nothing less.

You deserve to be honoured for valour if you are brave enough to ride a motorcycle through a lane known to be the abode of a dog. I wouldn't undertake this ride, even for a million dollars.

The dog catches the sound of your machine and spots the human cargo riding the strange contraption. Suddenly, its blood pressure rises. It gets an inflated idea of its importance. It growls, enquiring, "Hey, who enters my territory without my permission?" You have not received any training in the language of dogs and ignore the dog. This silence on your part enrages the dog which takes off on all fours, playing a symphony with howls from a raucous throat that reminds one of the 'Hound of the Baskervilles.'

The climax of the tragedy is reached when your motorcycle takes up the role of Judas and suddenly, develops engine trouble and comes to an abrupt stop. I cannot even imagine your plight when the unobliging mechanism makes you a target of attack of a blood-thirsty brute.

The inquisitiveness of a dog is monumental. I remember the strange experience of a friend. He had installed a radio and tuned it on when his dog, which was lying in sweet repose, got up. It viewed the radio with suspicious eyes, let out a vicious growl, and made a frantic dash at the radio. When my friend looked up, he saw the dog wagging its tail, awaiting its master to pat it for its successful fight with the intruder, the radio. Around him were strewn a few valves and splinters which once formed a radio.

Yet, the dog's desire to probe got one dog into serious trouble. Noticing a black cluster, almost inches from the ground, sticking to the stooping branch of a tree, the dog jumped at it and drove its teeth into the cluster.

Then it let out a deep moan and ran for dear life as a swarm of bees stung it angrily. Since then, this dog has kept away from all round, black objects. 'Once bitten, twice shy' holds true even for the members of the canine family.

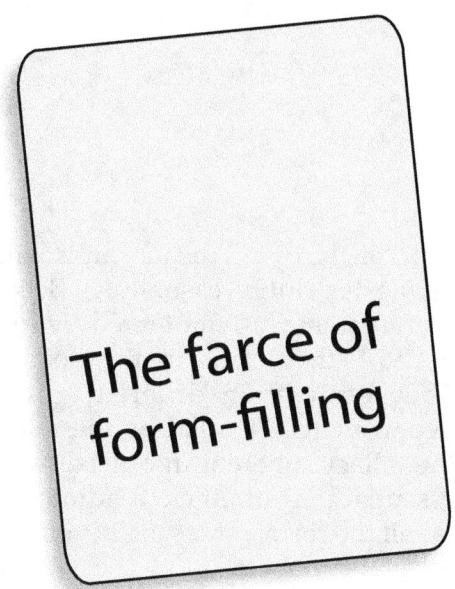

The farce of form-filling

THERE is an urgent need to liberate man from the tyrannical hold of forms. They are enervating, time-consuming, exasperating and irksome. And, last but not the least, these forms are distributed, filled up and filed away mechanically. Few of them ever get scrutinised.

This is the conclusion we draw after reading how Dean Rusk, one-time secretary of state of America, filled in a Federal employment form. He stopped for a moment at the line asking whether any relatives had ever plotted against the legal government and wrote, "Both my grandfathers served in the confederate army during the American civil war." It is unlikely that he would have been allowed to hold the high office he did if his form had been scrutinised.

Kingsley Martin had a similar experience. On his arrival at an Indian airport, he was given a health declaration form and was asked to fill up the details of where he spent each of the previous days before he arrived in India. While casually scrutinising the form before making the relevant entries, an idea suggested itself to the Editor of the *New Statesman*. He grinned to himself and filled in that one day ago, he was with Mary, two days ago with Suzanne, three days ago with Mabel and so on. Apparently, the form was taken from him by the official and filed away, unnoticed. The story leaked out when Kingslev Martin related it in his weekly magazine.

This is, by no means, an isolated instance of an official taking his duties casually. A Belgian businessman, Daniel Werwaecke, was smothered by forms. From the beginning of 1974, they came in the post, a dozen of them a day. They came from different government and municipal departments. Flooded by these forms and eager to expose the fallacy inherent in official thinking that forms form an essential part of efficient administration, Werwaecke filled up all the forms, showing his occupation as "Making masks for bank robbers."

He posted the forms, chuckling to himself. But he did not chuckle for long. In a few days, he began to receive enquiries from various departments in standard official letters. The departments asked him, "Do you grant discounts to wholesale dealers?"

The experience of French student, Jean Louviot, seems unbelievable but is authentic. He submitted his application for a passport in the form and instead of his own photograph, he affixed the photograph of his cocker spaniel. The passport authorities saw nothing wrong with the picture and the passport was duly issued. And for several months, Jean Louviot travelled through Europe. Not once did any official find a lack of resemblance between him and the photograph on the passport. When the story finally hit the Press, a red-faced customs border official commented, "It's the way kids wear their hair these days."

The trouble with forms is that often they have to be completed and attested too. In 1972, an illiterate trader of Vizag approached the State Bank for a loan of Rs. 200. He had to affix his left hand thumb impression at 132 places. His thumb must have been in a real battered condition when he finally walked out of the bank premises with the meagre loan.

These days, there is no form more menacing than the one sent out by the tax authorities. But to a well-known writer, the tax form is a source of creativity. He once noted, "I fill my tax return in the full knowledge that it is like my other work of fiction; the tax return inspires many to write stories in its columns."

IF PROVIDENCE would make me a dictator for just one day, I would pass an order prohibiting the practice of getting up from bed before the Sun has set out with its box of crayons to draw ribbons of crimson and red in the east.

So strong is my hatred for the dogma, 'Early to bed and early to rise make a man healthy and wealthy,' that I hold it to be the most obnoxious dictum handed over to us by our forefathers.

Many of us do not realise the advantage of lying in bed even after the cocks hail the dawn with their routine cries. The votaries of the early-to-rise precept claim that one has more time to attend to one's activities. What are these activities? Indulging in gossip that slanders the fair name of another. Smoking more cigars or gulping more cups of coffee, becoming enslaved to habits. Carrying out the dictates of the Lady of the House whose demands know no bounds. Bothering about the means to bridge the gap in the domestic budget which has the special knack of bloating itself into gigantic proportions, thanks to the spending spree of the family.

I remember the remark of a writer about the monthly budget: "I've too much month left at the end of my money." What for, I ask you, do you need more time? On the other hand, what a great charm the bed holds out for you if you are willing to embrace it with fervour and is ready to spend the major part of your time in sweet slumber. Cuddled up, with the knee caps almost touching your chin, you can dream of all the things that you can never hope to enjoy in real life.

You can have dates with colourful damsels, spinning and twisting on the gorgeous ballroom floor. You can see yourself in the role of a test cricketer, flogging the great speed merchant, Hall, or the crafty spin bowling of Benaud, scoring a century in your maiden test in a little over an hour. The more time you spend in bed, the farther your imagination gets to give shape to your aspirations and desires and to portray through dreams the fulfilment of the ambitions thwarted in life. Why should one get up early and miss the heartening scenes painted by dreams?

There is no greater pleasure on the face of this earth than enjoying the sweet hug of sleep. In the early morning, with a blanket loosely covering you, you feel transported to heaven.

When the first rays of the sun filter down through the window and spread the mellow light in the bedroom, making it difficult for you to continue your date with sleep, you can pull the blanket over the face, like a turtle hiding its head in its shell, and enjoy a few more hours of sleep.

Finally, you can get up from bed and derive the pride of belonging to the band of such renowned persons as Gerhardi who remarked, "I am not an early riser. The self respect which other men enjoy in rising early, I feel due to me for waking up at all." Discard the precept of early rising and become a devotee of the goddess of sleep. That is the only way to live a better life.

Do I hear someone saying, "The early bird gets the worm?" Indeed! But have you ever thought of the fate of the early-rising worm?

◆◆◆

Strangereasons

The ability to defend the indefensible goes hand in hand in with strange reasons. Those who have mastered this art do not bat an eyelid while they are asked to justify their conduct which flies against rhyme and reason. Instead, they assume an air of condescension while justifying their conduct, making it appear as if we must be real intellectual nincompoops not to have seen what they consider ought to be evident even to the meanest intelligence.

Who started this trend of reasoning which flies against reason, I don't know for certain. But the candidate, who comes closest to being the initiator is the great English humorist, A.P. Herbert. He did find some justification for beating a wife and noted:—*When Adam, day by day, Woke up in Paradise, He always used to say, Oh, this is very nice. But, Eve, from scene of Bliss Transported him for life. The more I think of this, The more I best my wife.*

This reminds one of an unbeatable competition which *The Spectator* organised some years back. Competitors were asked to file verses, giving strange reasons for their uncoinventional behaviour. Here are a few of the entries.

Leslie Johnson sang: *Who giveth alms, so we are told, shall be repaid a thousand fold. Alms giving, then, is not for me, I scorn the vice of usury.*

Dorothy Salmon defended her failure to maintain regular correspondence with friends:

The letter written,

Then the friends forgot; I'd friends remember, So I answer not.

Lakon popped up with a rather intelligent reply to someone who asked him why he did not turn up at church on Sundays:

Churches are places, I've heard people say,

Where sinners go to kneel and pray.

Shall I my reputation smirch, by being seen within the church?

Bushell loved to be in bed till late in the day. She ticked off someone who criticised her for being such a late-riser:

Ah, miracle of summer dawn! The tarnished world made new, the single lonely bird notes the meadows pale with dew Creations sixth fair morning, unmarked by human tread, promise I won't spoil it. I'll remain in bed.

Here are two amusing defences by fans of horse racing:

To wager is improvident; the sensible refuse to waste their money on a brute that's sure to go and lose! But how much more improvident and how much worse the sin, to fail to back a certainty and watch the blighter win!

The second plea by someone for his love for racing reads:

The bishops say I must not bet, nor buy a premium bond, Nor go in for the Football Pools of which I was so fond. But I may clothe the naked and love animals of course; so every week I mean to put my shirt on a horse.

And why did the horse—presumably the racing horse—bite the clergymen? Well, here is the excuse.

The steed bit his master. How came this to pass? He heard the good pastor cry,

All flesh is grass.

That bares to us some of the off-beat reasons presented by people who are adept at this fine art. That word *bares* takes me to a rather intelligent explanation that the American columnist, Erma Bombeck, put across. In reply to an invitation, she wrote back: "Yesterday, I received your colourful brochure and special invitation to be a guest at your nudist camp. I hope you will understand when I tell you that I must decline, as I don't have anything not to wear."

Secondfiddle

FROM whichever angle I examine it, I can find no flaws in the second fiddle. It looks to me exactly like the first fiddle .... the same shape, the same stretch of strings, the same willingness to have the bow glide over the strings.

Both the fiddles refuse to turn out soulful music when an untrained hand like, the one draws the bow. All that I get, whether I date the first fiddle or the second fiddle, are eerie notes. These notes have nothing musical in them. However much I try, the sounds fail to carry music in them. They leave jarring screeches and squeaks all around.

That opens my eyes to reality. There is no difference between the first fiddle and the second one. Or for that matter, the third fiddle or the fourth one.

Why, then, do we carry such a contempt for the second fiddle? How long can one stand and watch while the second fiddle is being mauled, sneered at, made an object of ridicule?

It is time we took a fresh look at the second fiddle. It becomes evident that the first fiddle dominates. It rides rough a shod over the second fiddle. Yet the first fiddle manages to make an impact only because the second one lays the base for the exotic notes. It is on the musical tracks defined by the second fiddle that the first one thrives.

Without the backing of the second fiddle, the first one will end up as a total failure, strike falesetto notes, tearing music to shreds. It is the second fiddle, the one that is dismissed disdainfully, which quietly, silently provides the sheet anchor for good music. Take away the second fiddle and the first one goes fumbling and stumbling.

The second fiddle knows all this. Yet it keeps a tight lip, lets a cloak of secrecy be spread over its prime role while the first fiddle corners all the credit.

The second fiddle is made to keep a low profile. It believes in selfless service and finds joy in helping the first fiddle gain name and fame. The readiness with which the second fiddle cuts itself off from the limelight has no parallel. The meek, they say, shall inherit the earth. If this be true, then it is the second fiddle, not the first fiddle, which will corner all the glory, one day.

Having played the second fiddle at home for over two decades, I have learnt its stabilising role. I know, from personal experience, that my wife plays the dominant notes, but the creative background for them is provided by me.

If I don't play the second fiddle, my wife finds herself left high and dry. Then she becomes morose, silent, withdrawn, ill at ease with herself. And she stays in pique till I provoke her, play the second fiddle, rouse her ire and make her play the dominant notes again.

It is clear, at least to me, that it is the person who handles the second fiddle who really matters. I hear King Nero chuckling merrily: "You said it, my friend. I fiddled for nearly a week, while Rome was burning. But it was not my fault. I could not stop playing the first fiddle so long as the notes of the second fiddle, the hiss and the buzz of the fire, egged me on."

◆◆◆

Amusing
Encounters

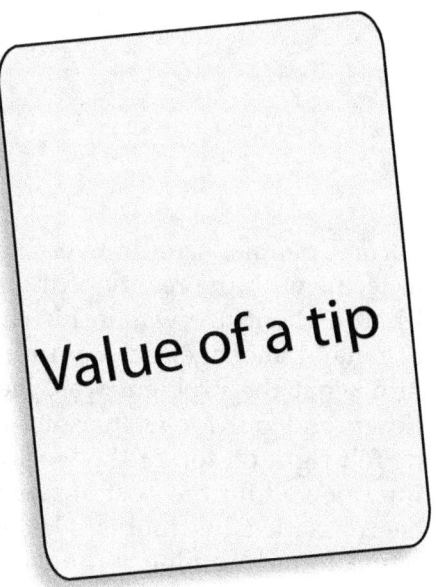

Value of a tip

Adi, (Dr Adimoolam, the eminent psychiatrist), and I are old classmates. We meet at the local club. We sit around a table, munch *pakoras* and sip hot coffee, lost in conversation till the grandfather clock strikes nine times, reminding us that it is 9 PM. "How time flies when one sits with a friend! Two hours have passed, yet we feel as if we just sat down to talk. Is that not yet another proof of Einstein's Theory of Relativity?" Adi grins. "We were lost in conversation," I respond. "The route that conversation takes is unpredictable. One topic leads to another and then to yet another one, skipping from one topic to the next, without striking any discordant note nor jerky motion, while time stands still," Adi's eyes gain a glint. "Aha," I choose to be brief. For I read in his eyes the hint that he has an interesting anecdote to share with me. "Conversation is essentially the product of the mind. Mind is ever restless, often in turmoil, rarely ever at peace with itself, and evokes comparison with a monkey that jumps from one branch to another, never accepting what is within reach, ever looking for what is not. But I am happy about that. If people learn to control the mind and thus, gain the ability to take the good and the bad in their stride, accept the mind, check their senses, be like the drop of water on a lotus leaf. And life shall never present a problem. No madness. No lunacy. No need to keep a date with a psychiatrist and his couch," Adi takes a break.

"If that happens, where will you go for a living?" I joke. "Most of my clients", he ignores my quip and continues, are normal people, sane in every way, yet unwilling to come to terms with the reality of the situation. A few days back, I had a client. He was in his early fifties, held the post of a general manager in a multinational company. I asked him what the problem was. He said he had been feeling down and out for no reason. Till a month back, said he, he felt right on top of the world. But since the day, he was interviewed for the post of senior general manager, he had been assailed by doubts. He feared that he might be left out. I found nothing wrong with him. Yet, I had to give him some tip. Suddenly, I remembered Peter's principles and level of incompetency. I told him that his problem was low self-esteem. It is very common among losers, I added, and advised him to recharge his self esteem. Once he did that, all would be well with him. The client bounced out of the couch, a big smile on his face. He shook hands with me, thanked me for identifying his trouble, gave me double my normal fees and left. I could not believe myself. I had told him nothing that anyone with common sense would not have offered him for free. In this world, anything that comes for free is considered worthless and hence, spurned. Value of a tip lies in the price, it commands, he ends; and thus, I find the moral of the story.

Apparatchik

"Do you know who the most hated man in our office is?" asks Suresh, a young man, the son of a close friend, working as a junior executive with a multinational. "How do I know? I am not on the rolls of your office. Nor am I good at guessing games," I joke. "I am talking of Kartik. He is my colleague. We joined the office, at the same time," Suresh says. "Why do you hate him? Is he proving to be better at work than you?," I prod him. "If that were the case, I would be jealous of him, I won't be hating him." "Aha." I choose to be brief. "I hate him. So do all of us, junior executives. Not one of them has a kind word for him," Suresh explains. "Is he an abominable NO MAN?" Is there an abominable No Man too? I had only heard of the abominable Snow Man," Suresh peers at me. "An abominable No Man is an employee who never sees Aye to Aye with anyone else," I pun. "You can't confer that title on him. He may say, NO to us, but he responds Aye to Aye to every observation of the boss. I have never seen him expressing a view different from that of the boss. He tows the lines, he draws, goes round and round the rut, behaving like the ox that works the oil mill in the village. Not once has he displayed a streak of independent thinking, original approach. We think of him as a boneless wonder." "Is he good at his work?" I ask. "I don't think so. He holds a desk with the lightest work load. He has a couple of hard working middle-aged clerks who do all the work. He shines in borrowed plumes. He signs their notes and reports with a flourish. He spends the rest of his time placating the boss, carrying tales about his colleagues. I think, he is blindly devoted to his superior in the organisation where he works," Suresh pauses. "That makes him the world's best Apparatchik?" "Apparatchik?" "Apparatchik refers to a team player but with negative connotations, Kartik is just that. An Apparatchik is a great conformist. He sticks to set practices and orders. He believes in the pecking order. Sometimes, he goes to extreme lengths to conform: I know one employee who has the company logo embroidered on his socks. There is another young man who, on the first day of spring, switches to light suits and pastel shirts," "I quote the definition of the Apparatchik that I had come across, a few days back." "Thank you. I shall share that term with my colleagues, make everyone call Kartik by the title Apparatchik, and bring him down by a notch or two," Suresh grins happily, indicating that his agony is abated.

Someone slaps you. You slap him back. That is 'tit for tat'. You pass on a counterfeit coin to the ice cream seller. He gives you an ice cream cone that has very little cream and sugar, more blotting paper. That is 'tit for tat.' We know several such cases of paying someone back in his own currency. That is how we get even with someone who pulls a fast one on us. But I am sure you would not have heard this story. An American couple sent their son to a residential school. The father paid all the dues to the school for one year. He promised his son a regular monthly grant. The boy was told that he should learn to meet his casual expenses within the grant amount. "Remember this, my son. The grant is yours. You can spend it as you like. I don't care if you spend it in one day; or spread it out over a month. I would be happy if you save part of it. Do what you will. I won't say a word. But, remember this too. You won't get a cent more, in any given month. You will have to make do with the grant, come what may," the father laid down the rules governing the grant. The boy nodded his head.

For a few months, the boy never overspent. Then came a special occasion. He did well in English at school, came out on top in the examination. His friends insisted that he hosted a special party to celebrate the occasion. He agreed. The month's grant got burnt out in one day. There still were ten days to the month. How could he manage without funds for ten days? Who would help him in the crisis? Who else but his father? Then he noticed how close the '$' sign is to the letter 'S'. That gave him a bright idea. He sat down, chuckling to himself, and mailed this letter: Dear Dad, school is really great. I am making lots of friends and studying very hard. With all my stuff, I simply can't think of anything I need, so if you would like, you can just send me a card, as I would love to hear from you. Love, Your son.

    The father sensed what the boy wanted. He was in NO mood to oblige. He too knew how to convey that message to his son. He wrote back: Dear Son, I kNOw that astroNOmy, ecoNOmics, and oceaNOgraphy are eNOugh to keep an hoNOurs student busy. Do NOt forget that the pursuit of kNOwledge is a Noble task, and you can never study eNOugh. Love. Your NO Nonsense Papa. This exchange of letters, in my view, is a classical case of 'tit for tat'.

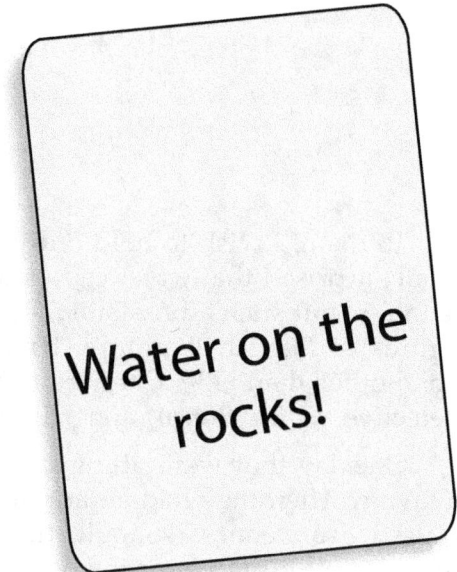

Water on the rocks!

Believe it or not, water intoxicates. One cannot only get drunk on it, behave tipsily and go around groggily, but even drink oneself to death.

I hear a thousand men and women raising their vocal chords, shouting and screaming, charging me with pillorying the only drink that doesn't have the killer instincts. They admit that water often carries deadly germs, but, then, water, at best, can only be charged with being an accessory to the crime. Water, they affirm, never kills.

How wrong they can be?

Is not water in the lungs which causes chest congestion and prepares the scene for dangerous maladies? How about the stranglehold which water exercises when someone who doesn't know swimming gets beyond his depths? Or finds himself unable to swim for long because the distance he has to cover to reach the shore is far beyond the physical strength he has?

Now comes a report which says that one can drink oneself to death on water.

The *Independent* of London carries a story about such a bizarre incident. 20-year-old, Andrew Naylor, a night-club reveller, drank himself to death. He downed more than 20 pints of water after taking a tablet of the drug, *Ecstasy*. This caused his body to heat up. He died from brain damage caused by water intoxication.

My critics are suddenly silenced.

To them, I wish to hold out yet another fact. I am not at all surprised that water causes intoxication. I have been taught about such a possibility, years ago, by two eminent figures of English literature. I remember that lesson, by none other than G.K. Chesterton. (He created the famous detective, *Father Brown*) and Hilaire Belloc.

One day, they were sitting and enjoying heady spirits at a tavern. Then they had an argument. They debated what caused drunkenness? Should the blame squarely rest on the whisky or the gin or the brandy, they consumed. They could not arrive at a firm conclusion. Then an idea came to them. They agreed to carry out experiments with different forms of liquor during the next few days. On the first day, they drank whisky and water. They got drunk.

It was the turn of gin and water on the second day. And, lo presto, once again, their heads were heavy and their steps were unsteady when they called it a day.

Brandy and water came in on the third day. The two drank glass after glass till they could not even stand up.

After this experiment, they knew, for certain, the culprit. When they met, next day, having recovered from the effects of the drink, they were sober. They could analyse the results with clarity.

It did not take them long to realise that one element was common. Water had been added to whisky, on the first day; to gin, on the second day; and to brandy, on the third day. On all the three occasions, they had got drunk.

There was no doubt, then, in their minds that the blame should rest squarely on water. That conclusion has now been buttressed by the sad tale of Naylor.

A dozen young boys and girl grin at me when I open the door in response to the insistent buzz made by the bell. I stand, framed against he door, and enquire: "Ah...yes... What can 1 do for you".

"Morning, sir... We are from the Youth Association. We are arranging a meeting on the 10th of this month. We will be glad if you can speak to us. We want to hear your views on any topic you choose, anything that will make us a little more enlightened," says a lanky youth of 20 summers while friends cast smiles at me, confident of winning me over.

"Why pick on me? I am a virtual nobody," I decide to wriggle out of this commitment, if possible. "Ah... sir... Don't put on that cloak of non-entity," coos a girl, with a bright smile and a confident mien, "We have read your humorous articles in major newspapers and magazines. We know how to create ripples of laughter with ease. That is why we want you. You are a sort of hero to us. Some of us hold the view that this nation need not have any fears about the future so long as there are people like you who can see the funny side of life. That makes you an obvious choice, as the speaker for the occasion."

That term 'Obvious' triggers a spark of memory. I remember the use to which the late King George V of Britain, then the Prince of Wales, put the word, 'Obvious' to handle a similar situation. That gives me a very naughty idea. I stare at the youngsters and comment: "So, when it comes to humour, I am an obvious person."

"You said it, sir," the boys and the girls chime, in chorus.

"When is the function?" I enquire.

"At 4p.m. on 10th September. The venue is the Assembly Hall of the YMCA. We shall pick you up, sir..." the girl who had talked about the term 'Obvious' replies.

"So you are a sort of pickpocket. Only, you don't bother to use blades. You lift the person, who has a dress that has pockets, so you can empty the contents of all the pockets at leisure... But, maybe I am not that easily pickable... Since you have made a process of pick and choose, I shall choose to come there on my own. I hope that too is obvious, since I am your obvious choice," I play with words.

"As you like it, sir... You use words with great skill," the girl pays me a compliment. Then the group greets me once again, and departs.

I reach the venue of the meeting. I am welcomed warmly, garlanded and led to the rostrum. The proceedings begin. The president of the Youth Association takes his seat by my side. One of the members delivers the welcome address. He details the achievements of the Youth League. Then he lists my so-called role in setting new trend, in humorous writing. The president then invites me to speak.

I take my place behind the mike. I smile, at the hundred odd people, mostly young boys and girls, who are present. The hall is full. I thank the organisers for inviting me to speak on any subject of my choice. And then I begin, "I thought I can do no better than define myself clearly. One of you, when you extended the invitation to me to speak here, on this occasion, told me that I am your obvious choice. You seem to be unaware of the true meaning of the word 'Obvious'. I am supposed to be an 'Obvious' choice. That makes me an 'Obvious' person. So, I would live up to that title 'Obvious' person. I shall not veer away from the right definition of the word 'Obvious'. 'Obvious' means 'Goes Without Saying'. I, being an 'Obvious' person, too, shall go without saying," and resume my seat, while the stunned audience takes a few seconds to appreciate the tenor of my speech and rents the hall with a thunderous ovation.

Fattening thoughts

"Hi... What has happened to you? You have bloated up, like a balloon," I sneer at my friend Shankar, whom I meet after nearly five years.

"You are like a beanstalk. How can you ever get a measure of the pleasure which is reserved for the man who is fat and stout and well filled." Shankar counters, with glee.

"You mean the fat adipose into which you have turned is an image with which you vibe well," I express my surprise.

"Why not?"

"Don't you know that people deride the fat man as one who lives on the fat of the land," I pop up with one reason which offers discomfiture to anyone who is rotund.

"Who doesn't live on the fat of the land? It is the earth that feeds us all. It is the earth that feeds every living thing. The food chain, which provides the equilibrium so that no species grows beyond the limits of tolerance by making each form of life, food for another species, itself is a sure indication that everything that has life finally gets sustenance from the land. Understand?" Shankar demolishes my theory with a sly smile.

"My God! You seem to be enjoying your fatty form," I comment.

"Why not?"

"But, why," I enquire.

"Because stability is where I am. The thin man can be swept off even by the flimsiest of wind. But, even a typhoon shall fail to take the fat one for a ride," Shankar answers.

"And."

"You don't believe this stability theory," Shankar notices a lack of conviction in my reaction and asks.

"Honestly, I don't."

"Then you don't know Bhage Gobbardan well," Shankar drops the name of the MP, who began with the JD (S), but changed to the Congress fold later.

"Of all the people whose name you could have dropped, you could only pick on a relatively unknown one," I carp.

"But, I do it with valid reason. On April 16, 1991, when asked why he had joined the Congress, the fat, massive politician from Orissa stated, "Wherever I go, there is stability." He said it before the elections of 1991. How prophetic his prediction turned out to be!

"I see."

"There are other reasons why you should respect a man who is fat," Shankar adds.

"Like..."

"Fat men have a sense of humour. You could not have forgotten the ebullient wit in our parliament, the late Piloo Mody," Shankar points out.

"One swallow..."

"I know that cliche, so you don't have to complete it, "Shankar cuts in, before adding, "Fat men are polite too. William Howard Taft, one-time President of the United States, was very fat. He weighed over 300 lbs. He was hailed as one of the politest men of all ages. For, by rising from his seat, he enabled three people to sit."

"That's a real joke."

"I admit."

And, once, Taft got a train to make an unscheduled stop at a wayside station, by sending out a message that the halt was essential to take a large party on. When the train official found only Taft, ready to board, he asked, "Where is the large party?" Taft took his seat, while explaining to the official, "Can't you see, I am the large party." "Need I say anything more," Shankar concludes, leaving me speechless by the logic of his words.

Clock watch

"HI... What are you gaping at?" My friend Adityan pats me, gently, when he spots me, sitting in my cubicle, my eyes riveted on the wall-clock which seems to have gone off into a state of stupor. "The wall-clock. It is not ticking on. It has gone into a state of hibernation. It has got stuck at 4.45..." I grumble.

"You have a clock which is better than the watch I possess," says Adityan, forcing me to sit up. "That is ridiculous. How can you ever assert that a clock which is not working is better than a watch which is working?" I indicate that his words fail to make sense.

"Quite simple, my dear ..Your clock is stuck at 4.45... So, it will show the right time twice a day. Once at 4.45 am, and again at 4.45 pm. But, my accursed watch, which gains two minutes everyday, never shows the right time. Not even once a day," Adityan laughs, assuming that he has cracked a joke.

"I am not amused," I lean back in my seat and grumble.

"Oh, oh... How can you be so depressed, just because the clock has stopped... Or, my dear... are you a clock watcher?... You sit in the office, but your eyes are ever on the clock. Your mind keeps a track of time. You calculate, every time, how much more time you have to spend dating files and papers and communications. You are naturally upset because the clock is no longer working," Adityan snaps at me.

"Oh no... If that were the case, I would have been booted out, long time back. But, here I am, somewhere at the middle level, with hopes of rising further in the hierarchy," I counter his comment.

"Since that reflects the situation, why are you so morose and upset over the clock which is not working?" Adityan does not seem to understand my plight.

"Once upon a time, one could wind the clock. That was a pleasure. I learnt while winding the clock, every week, that one can't put the clock back.. backwardness is not for clocks. They are ever on an onward march. The sands of time keep grinding fine... but one can at least wind the clock. But even this has become obsolete. Now, I can't even wind the clock. Not the clock that has taken into its silly head that it need not continue to move along with time. In the good old days, I would have immediately rushed to wind it and to force it to tick again. But, this clock does not work on the spring system," I mumble.

"Aha..." Adityan fails to see what I have in mind. This is a clock which works on battery... a quartz clock which gets the energy to move its second, minute and hour hands from tiny battery cells... penlight batteries, in many cases. Though I can't understand the origin of the term, Penlight.. You can't use them as writing instruments; nor do they throw light except when they slip into torchlights. Now, the battery of this clock has run down. Unless new battery is introduced, the clock will remain idle.

"And God only knows how long the stores will take to supply the battery. For, the stores, almost always, have a pet answer. 'The item demanded is not presently in stock.

Indent has been placed and the item will be supplied as soon as it is received'. So, I am sure this clock will remain idle for quite sometime now... From watching modern timekeeping equipment, I realise that I can't put the clock back; nor can I wind it. I can only recharge it.. Or, perhaps, even that, I can't do. Only the battery can," I conclude.

Silencing the wag

To Raghav, playing with words comes naturally. He does that every time, a chance comes his way through a casual remark made to him or said in his presence. Once he spots the chance, he turns into a tiger on the hunt. His eyes gain a gleam; his lips flutter; his body speaks the language of a killer. Words flow, out of him, as if the sluice gate of the Bhakra Dam has suddenly been raised.

They make me hot and sizzling, like the lava of a volcano that has stirred itself out of deep slumber. They sweep everyone around with the speed and power of an avalanche. Hopefully, some day, scientists may work out a way to prevent natural avalanches, but have a hunch that they will never succeed in curbing the tumble of words that Raghav's tongue releases every time it gets a chance to express itself.

So I keep my tongue under tight rein when Raghav is anywhere around. But, today, Raghav walks in while I am telling Vijay, my colleague, that by mistake, I bit the tip of my tongue and it is hurting. I push the tongue out for Vijay to assess the damage.

"How unbecoming of a man to put his tongue out at a colleague," I hear a voice, turn and spot Raghav heading toward us, crinkling with laughter. Then he inquires what the problem is. I reluctantly share with brim the secret of my pain.

"It is not grave enough to leave you tongue-tied," he examines the sore and condiments.

"Is not the tongue always tied?" I ask.

"Not at both ends. Its free end holds the wag," jokes Raghav.

"At the moment, you are wagging your tongue," I snap. But it skids off his back like a stone that frog-leaps on the placid waters of a pool."

"Can't help it, my, friend. The throat is the source of words and of divine music too. Rightly has the vibrating reed of a musical instrument been named its tongue," he says.

"I hear warnings. I am afraid you are going to bore me to death with an overdose of verbal play," I contort my face in mock fear.

"Rings are expected where the tongue is. The gong of a bell is called its tongue. When the gong swings—swing is another word for wag—and hits the bell's main frame, rings are produced," Raghav lets a smile touch his lips, before his eyes fall on my shoes.

"The tongue of your right shoe is visible," he says.

"The shoe has a tongue?" I am taken aback.

"Yes. The piece of leather that bridges the gap between the flaps of the shoe drawn together by the lace is called the tongue. Tighten the lace," he tells me.

"My God!" I stoop and tighten the lace so that the flaps wrap up the tongue and make it invisible.

"You have made the shoe tongue-tied," Raghav cracks a joke.

"Have you said it all?" I throw up my hand in sheer exasperation. "Oh, no," he grins and continues, "Children often find delight in challenging us to repeat tongue-twisters. Ah, there is a very interesting insight into the tongue," suddenly his pace slows down. He gropes around, unable to pin down the thought that seems to be at the tip of his tongue.

"Raghav! Wise people know when to hold their tongues. Now is the time for you to act wise," I silence him with that sharp reproof and make myself scarce before he finds his voice.

For friendship's sake

I'm carefully counting the notes—twenty hundred-rupee notes handed over to me by the teller, after he has ensured that my account does have enough balance and compared my signature, a dozen times with those I left on the bank's records to convince himself that I am indeed who I claim to be, when I hear a call, "Ah, Krish. I went to your house and was told by your wife that you'd gone to the bank."

"And you tracked me down?" I count the notes, assure myself that I have got the amount I had signed for, tuck the notes in the purse and slip the cash into the shirt pocket, before responding to Bhir Singh Burena, a colleague and friend.

"You draw me unto you like a magnet drawing an iron filing," Burena has the skill to turn out similes, and he doesn't wait for even the proverbial drop of the hat to do that.

"Don't tell that to my wife. Or, she may rush to the conclusion that we're gays," I joke.

"That's what I like about you. You spot the funny side of things, readily," he pads up to me.

"Aha," I smell a rat.

"Believe me, Krish. When it comes to humour, you are not a wee bit less masterly than, say, Art Buchwald or Rajinder Puri or V Gangadar," he now takes to dropping names.

"Wish the rest of the world shares your view," I pout my lips, indicating the reservations that swell within.

"It will. It's just a matter of time," Burena drops his voice and adds, "Well, I'm in a little bit of trouble."

"Is the water hot enough to make you uncomfortable?" I tease him before asking, "What's the problem? And where do I come into the picture?"

"I have to pay the electricity charges... about nine hundred rupees, today. Otherwise, the cussed lineman will disconnect the line, and leave me and my family in utter darkness. But I do not have ready money. That's where you can help me. I shall return the amount, on the first. The moment I lay my hand on the pay packet," Burena is persuasive.

"Sorry, my friend. I can't help you. I've drawn just Rs 2,000 because my account doesn't hold more. I've on hand an outlay of about Rs 2,500; so I still need Rs 500 to tide over the fiscal pressure," I dodge.

"Have a heart, Krish!" the man virtually croons.

"I do have a heart, but it acts under the dictates of my mind. The mind says that charity begins at home. Since the funds, I've are needed by me, I've to politely and regretfully turn down your appeal for a loan," I make my meaning clear.

"Where does that leave me?" Burena wrings his hands.

"It gives you the tip that it's time to find another soul, ready to loosen the purse-strings after hearing your sob story," I joke.

"This is no laughing matter," Burena glows with fury.

"You said that I have a highly evolved sense of humour. Laughter abides where the wit rules high," I parry.

"So I don't get the loan?" Burena's tone is one of utter helplessness.

"Sorry, my friend. I want you to remain my friend. Forever, if I can help it. And a loan is the last thing that helps a friendship flourish. Listen to this proverb from Portugal: 'If you want to make an enemy, lend a man money and ask it of him,' I stop on finding Burena scurrying out of my presence, creating the impression that a pack of hounds are after his blood.

Right logic

Who can delve into the thoughts of another! No one.

I am pretty sure of that. In fact, when I look at myself, I find that there are many conflicting personalities in my psyche. I am more than one person, myself. And I have not got a full measure of my strengths and weaknesses, of the many types of Jekylls and Hydes, lurking within, each one waiting for the right moment to find expression.

This thought strikes me when I learn that my friend, Sudhir, a smart and graceful old main of sixty, a confirmed bachelor is getting married. I get the information through a card which arrives in the day's post, inviting me to witness the function.

The news leaves me flabbergasted.

Often, had I heard Sudhir subtly side-stepping my suggestion to get married. He had skirted the issue with all the diplomatic skill of which he is capable. (He had recently retired from the Foreign office, and had gone round world capitals, a number of times; at times for, quite a few years). He would tell me, "What is the hurry?" Or, laugh it off, "Who knows, I may not be destined to marry." Or, nudge me and say, "Have you got a girl in mind?"

By such reactions, Sudhir had given me the impression that he has found his pot of joy, by being footloose and fiancee-free. So the sudden decision to get into wedlock, at this late age, shocked me. Who is the girl that has cast her spell on him, melted his declared determination to go it alone in life and forced him to slip the ring on her finger? I take the first available opportunity to drop in at his place.

He welcomed me with a big smile. Playing the host, he sets before me a plate, laden with pastries and biscuits. He barks out, to his Jeeves, "Ho coffee, please." He knows that I am a teetotaller. That explains why he refrains from turning to the choicest of wines, he has in stock.

"How are you? Must be feeling right on top of the world?" I ask, when we settle down on the setee.

"May be," he ducks a direct answer.

"Who is the girl?"

"Wait till my wedding day. You shall be there. She is not a girl. She is around 40. So..." Sudhir leaves the sentence midway in the air.

"Now, tell me, what have you found in the... "I stopped short of the word 'girl', slipping out. Then I said, 'Lady'.

"Nothing special."

"Then why have you decided to marry?"

"The reason is easily perceptible. There are two types of women on this globe; Marriage is a lottery because no fool-proof method to categorise any woman, in advance, is as yet available.—Once you concede this fact, the reason shall be readily apparent," says Sudhir. "I can't make head or tail of your logic." I admit.

"Well, if she turns out to be a nag, I won't have to live with her for long. But if she is kind and understanding, she was worth waiting for", Sudhir has a very convincing argument about his decision to enter matrimony, late.

www.ingramcontent.com/pod-product-compliance
Lightning Source LLC
Chambersburg PA
CBHW070317230426
43663CB00011B/2164